40/50

PF/370

D1374470

CARRIER OPERATIONS IN WORLD WAR II

Volume One   —   —   The Royal Navy

CARRIER OPERATIONS IN WORLD WAR II

Volume One
The Royal Navy

J. D. Brown

LONDON

IAN ALLAN

© IAN ALLAN 1968

7110 0040 9

Published in the United Kingdom by Ian Allan Ltd., Shepperton, Surrey and printed by Netherwood Dalton & Co. Ltd., Huddersfield, Yorkshire.

Contents

Foreword

by Vice Admiral Sir Donald Gibson, KCB, DSC
FLAG OFFICER, NAVAL AIR COMMAND

THIS book recounts in a matter of fact way the operations of the British Aircraft Carriers in World War II. The author has stuck to the facts, and names of individuals are seldom if ever mentioned, nevertheless, it stirs the blood.

There is a lesson to be learned on every other page, and if one had to choose a motto for it the one word FLEXIBILITY would be enough.

I am very delighted to have been asked to write a foreword to this book by the author, who has made a significant contribution to military history. The quiet and competent manner in which he has told these great stories does honour to the Fleet Air Arm in which both he and I are privileged to serve.

Acknowledgements

Acknowledgements are due to the following individuals, who have most generously loaned photographs from their private collections, or have dug back into their log-books or memories to give me the background to many of the events recorded in this book:

D. J. Frearson, Esq.
R. J. Jones, Esq.
C. F. Shores, Esq.
W. T. Speary, Esq.
A. J. Ward, Esq.

Commander T. L. M. Brander, DSC, Royal Navy
Commander I. J. Davies, DSC, RN

Surgeon Commander W. A. N. Mackie, DSC, MB, ChB, RN

Commander R. H. Reynolds, DSC, RN
Commander H. S. M. Wilkins, MBE, RN (Retd)

Lieutenant Commander J. W. Armstrong, RN
Lieutenant Commander W. J. Curtis, RN (Retd)
Lieutenant Commander F. W. Dodd, RN
Lieutenant Commander I. J. Gilman, RN
Lieutenant Commander C. Hearnshaw, DSM, RN
Lieutenant Commander F. Rodgers, RN
Lieutenant Commander P. J. Spelling, RN
Lieutenant Commander T. E. J. St Vaughan, MBE, RN
Lieutenant Commander Van der Minne, Royal Netherlands Navy
Lieutenant Commander L. A. Cox, RN (Retd)

Lieutenant R. Priestly-Cooper, RN
Lieutenant D. R. Whittaker, RN
Lieutenant G. J. N. Wood, RN

and, of course, E. C. Hine, Esq., of the Imperial War Museum staff, who was so helpful in the search for fresh material. Many other people have assisted in the preparation of this book, in a variety of ways: I should like to extend my thanks to them all.

J. D. Brown

Weymouth, Dorset
August 1968

Introduction

IN less than six years the Fleet Air Arm grew from a small striking force, limited in numbers, manpower and material, to a powerful strategic weapon, with a minimum of non-combatant units, which was as large as the pre-War Royal Air Force in terms of effective front-line aircraft. Conceived and initially employed as an extension of the big guns of the Fleet, naval aviation was developed to the point where the aircraft carrier became the vital ship in any formation, offensive or defensive, with the battleship providing anti-aircraft protection with its considerable medium and close-range batteries.

The roles of the carrier aircraft were those traditionally fulfilled by the Royal Navy, only the method and time-factor differing. The primary tasks were the destruction of enemy fleets; offensive and defensive patrol, search, and reconnaissance; offensive operations to seek out and destroy enemy shipping in coastal waters and harbours, and also to strike at accessible shore installations; the support and protection of seaborne landings.

The list of major warships sunk or seriously damaged by the naval aircraft is impressive, although the caution with which the German and Italian Navies employed their surface fleets when opposed by the Home and Mediterranean Fleets led to fewer encounters than might have been expected. The battleships LITTORIO, VITTORIO VENETO, CAIO DUILIO, RICHELIEU and DUNKERQUE were all torpedoed and put out of action by Swordfish and Albacore aircraft between June 1940 and May 1941, while BISMARCK and CONTE DI CAVOUR were sunk through naval air action in the same period, together with the heavy cruisers POLA, ZARA and FIUME. After March 1942, when TIRPITZ survived a torpedo attack by Albacores, there were no further attacks by Fleet Air Arm strike aircraft on major warships at sea, apart from a single dive-bombing attack on the Japanese cruiser HAGURO in May 1945.

In the absence of enemy fleet operations on the high seas, the carriers mounted air strikes against the harbours from April 1940 until the closing days of the War. After an initial failure at Trondheim the aircraft went on to improve their techniques 'and to gain experience. Taranto was an outstanding example of a highly effective attack achieved with the minimum resources, while, at the other end of the scale, the sustained intensity of the final operations over the Japanese Home Islands clearly demonstrated that carrier forces, armed with the best available aircraft, could successfully wage a war of attrition against a modern nation.

Not only maritime targets were attacked: a vast amount of damage was inflicted on airfields, road and rail systems and shipyards during the last month of the War, by nearly 2,000 aircraft from a score of American and British carriers.

The search and reconnaissance potential of the Fleet Air Arm was fully realized in the trade protection role, particularly in the highly specialized anti-submarine warfare. The early adoption of Air to Surface Vessel radar by the Royal Navy for its aircraft, coupled with the existing expertise in night and bad weather operations, gave the Fleet Air Arm a lead in this field which was maintained until the end of the War. In addition to the operations against surface and submarine raiders, the aircraft carriers took part in some of the fiercest air battles of the War, in defense of merchant convoys. The limited number of fighters available at any one time prevented any of the convoys from being completely overwhelmed by enemy air attack and indeed on only one occasion were appreciable losses inflicted on a convoy protected by naval fighters—PQ18 in September 1942.

Carrier-based aircraft supported every major amphibious operation from the landings in Norway in April 1940 through to the re-occupation of Singapore in September 1945, with the sole exception of the evacuation of Dunkirk, although even there the land-based Skuas and Swordfish were deeply committed. The cover provided by the naval aircraft was indispensable wherever the beach-head was at or beyond the limit of shore-based air cover and without this form of support many of the landings would have been impracticable. In the Pacific, where the United States Navy carried the principles involved in amphibious operations to the ultimate, the entire prosecution of the War depended upon sea/air power and without the powerful carrier task forces for both distant striking and inshore support victory would have been won at an almost unacceptable cost in life and material.

The expansion of the Fleet Air Arm was not accomplished without difficulties being experienced in both manpower and aircraft procurement. The shortage of personnel was most marked in 1941 and 1942, the years when the original aircrews and maintenance personnel had become casualties or were employed on training the "second" generation, who did not become fully operational until mid-1943. A very high percentage of the aircrew officers were drawn from the Volunteer Reserves, not only of Great Britain, but also in particular Canada, New Zealand and South Africa; the ratio of VR to regular officers in the TIRPITZ strike of April 1944 was 138 to 25. The shortage of ground crews was never really met and their successful efforts to maintain a high standard of serviceability in the front-line squadrons was above praise.

Aircraft procurement presented even more problems. Until the advent of adequate supplies of American aircraft from June 1943, the Fleet Air Arm was obliged to fight with small numbers of out-performed aircraft, some types being adapted from standard Royal Air Force equipment. Not until the formation of the first Corsair squadron did the Royal Navy possess an aircraft equal to any contemporary fighter. Owing to the pre-occupation of the larger part of the British aircraft industry with the production of RAF aircraft, the only naval aircraft of indigenous design to see combat after June 1940 were the Fairey Barracuda and the Fairey Firefly; the former could hardly be classed as an outstanding design, while the latter was too slow for its designed role. Although Sea Hurricanes and Seafires were delivered to the Fleet Air Arm in large numbers, such conversions could not hope to meet all the stringent requirements for full carrier operations and while they gave invaluable service, *faut de mieux*, they compared unfavourably with contemporary aircraft designed for the task.

At the beginning of May 1940, five aircraft carriers were operational with the Royal Navy, of which two were in action with less than 80 aircraft embarked. Five years later, at the beginning of May 1945, 16 Fleet and escort carriers were at sea with over 500 aircraft embarked. Another dozen carriers were on passage to combat areas or in the final stages of working-up, with nearly 400 aircraft embarked.

This book deals with the operations of aircraft flying from the aircraft carriers. Reference to the invaluable effort supplied by Fleet Air Arm units ashore has been kept to a minimum because of restrictions of space. The shore-based squadrons, usually under Royal Air Force operational control, made a major contribution to the maritime defence of Great Britain and of overseas coastal areas. Not only did they carry out routine anti-submarine patrols and fighter patrols over coastal waters, but a continual offensive was maintained against enemy shipping and warships. One such operation was 825 Squadron's heroic attack on the SCHARNHORST, GNEISENAU and PRINZ EUGEN in February 1942, for which Lieutenant Commander E. Esmonde's leadership earned him a posthumous Victoria Cross.

The activities of the catapult-armed warships are mentioned in passing, not because any lack of achievement, but for the reason given above for the shore-based squadrons. With the shortage of carriers up to 1943, the Seafoxes, Walrus and Kingfishers were often the only aircraft available, albeit in small numbers, in ocean waters, searching for disguised raiders and blockade runners.

A subsequent volume will deal with the work of the Fleet Air Arm units not engaged directly in aircraft carrier operations, but which contributed so much to the fine operational record of the Fleet Air Arm during World War II.

Section 1

THE ATLANTIC AND ARCTIC

OCEAN WARFARE: September 1939 to March 1940

Following the outbreak of War on 3rd September 1939, the aircraft carriers which were available to the Home Fleet were deployed for anti-submarine patrols, ARK ROYAL in the North West Approaches, COURAGEOUS and HERMES in the South West Approaches. As the convoy system had not been introduced so early in the War, the carriers simply flew off searches in the areas of probable U-boat activity. The first indication that such tactics were dangerous for the carriers came on 14th September, when U-39 very nearly hit ARK ROYAL. Destroyers of the carrier's screen sank the U-boat, but that afternoon the inadequacy of the aircraft weapons was demonstrated—two Skuas of 803 Squadron were lost to the explosion of their own bombs while attacking U-30, the U-boat surviving the attack and rescuing the pilots of both aircraft.

Just three days later COURAGEOUS was sunk, with heavy loss of life, by U-29, despite the fact that the ship's Swordfish were airborne throughout the time that the U-boat was working into an attacking position. The two screening destroyers failed to sink the U-boat, which returned safely to Germany. The loss came as a clear indication that the carriers were unsuited for anti-submarine warfare at the then current state of the art, and the sweeps were abandoned.

With the knowledge that at least one pocket-battleship was at large in ocean waters the five remaining carriers were despatched to form the nuclei of various raider hunting groups. FURIOUS was employed for most of the winter on escort duties in the North Atlantic, accompanied by the battlecruiser REPULSE, protecting the important troop convoys sailing between Halifax (Nova Scotia) and the Clyde. The West Indies were covered by HERMES and the modern French battleship STRAS-BOURG, moving to Dakar in early 1940. In the Indian Ocean GLORIOUS patrolled the Aden entrance to the Red Sea, while EAGLE covered the trade routes that converge on the East Indies. The only Force to see positive success, Force K, was built around ARK ROYAL and RENOWN. ARK ROYAL took part in just one more operation with the Home Fleet after her narrow escape from the U-boat, and in the course of a brief sortie into the North Sea her Skuas shot down the first German aircraft to be destroyed by British forces, a Do 18 shadower, on 25th September 1939.

11

DISPOSITION OF VESSELS AND SQUADRONS

North and South Atlantic Trade Protection

ARK ROYAL

800 Squadron	9 Skuas	
803 „	9 Skuas (to end of September 1939)	
810 Squadron	12 Swordfish	
820 „	12 Swordfish & 1 Walrus	
821 „	12 Swordfish	

FURIOUS

801 Squadron	9 Skuas
816 „	9 Swordfish
818 „	9 Swordfish

COURAGEOUS — sunk 17th September 1939 by U-29

811 Squadron	12 Swordfish
822 „	12 Swordfish

HERMES

814 Squadron	12 Swordfish (transferred from ARK ROYAL 4th September, 1939)

ALBATROSS — (based at Hastings, Freetown from October 1939)

710 Squadron	6 Walruses

EAGLE & GLORIOUS — See under Indian Ocean

Over a period of four months the nine Swordfish squadrons in the five ships searched about six million square miles of ocean. The majority of the huge effort yielded negative results, which were of value in that they showed at least where the enemy was *not*. As mentioned above, the only Force to find the enemy was that which included ARK ROYAL, with her larger aircraft complement. In October 1939 her Swordfish sighted, but failed to identify, the notorious ALTMARK, one of the GRAF SPEE's supply ships. In the following month, however, they found and stopped the SS UHENFELS, to be boarded and taken in prize by the destroyers of Force K. Operating between Cape Verde and Pernambuco, ARK ROYAL and her consorts were in a favourable position to intercept any German vessel, warship or blockade-runner attempting to return to Europe; in December Force K's presence was threat enough to have a major influence upon the decision to scuttle GRAF SPEE off Montevideo on 17th of that month.

After the destruction of the only surface raider *known* to be at large, the composition and disposition of the hunting groups were re-arranged. HERMES and STRASBOURG were moved to the Dakar-Freetown area to supplement the local patrols flown by ALBATROSS' Walrus aircraft and to provide the only deep cover at this focal point of trade. GLORIOUS continued to patrol the approaches to the Red Sea until the middle of January 1940, when she returned to the Mediterranean Fleet; EAGLE left her station off the East Indies to enter Singapore dockyard for a re-fit.

While ARK ROYAL was returning to the United Kingdom in February 1940 she participated in a search for blockade-runners off the coast of Spain, where her Swordfish found five of the six enemy merchant ships attempting to return to Germany. By now aware of the menace of this ship, the U-boat High Command laid an unsuccessful trap for ARK as she was returning through the Bay of Biscay.

The sustained flying through the winter months were an invaluable work-up for the events which were soon to follow. This applied particularly to the planning staffs, which had shown themselves capable of putting into effect operations far from the complex base organisations to be found in the United Kingdom and Malta. While the aircrew were afforded excellent practice in the difficult arts of long-range search and navigation, other aspects of their roles were of necessity neglected, and the lack of current practice in the delivery of the highly specialised torpedo strike was demonstrated in later operations.

NORWAY — 1940

When the German invasion of Norway commenced on 9th April 1940, the only carrier in Home Waters was FURIOUS, re-fitting in the Clyde. She cut short her re-fit and sailed on 10th to join the Home Fleet but so little time was available that she left behind her Skua squadron, with the result that the Fleet and the first contingent of the Allied Army ashore were without fighter cover for the first fortnight of the campaign.

ARK ROYAL was training aircrew off Gibraltar at this time, but 15 Skuas of her 800 and 803 Squadrons, left behind at Hatston in the Orkneys to supplement the local defences, undertook a dive-bombing strike on the cruiser KOENIGSBERG at Bergen on 10th April. Operating at maximum range the Skuas took the defences by surprise and sank their target with three 500lb bomb hits and many near-misses, for the loss of just one Skua. The raid was remarkable in that it was the first to result in the destruction of a major enemy surface vessel by aircraft alone.

On the following day, 11th April, Swordfish from FURIOUS carried out the first large-scale torpedo attack, against two destroyers in Trondheimfjord. The strike was not a success, principally because of lack of knowledge of the area, and most of the torpedoes grounded in shallow water. The Swordfish subsequently took part in both Battles of Narvik and were very active in the strike and reconnaissance roles, providing the only air support for the Allied Expeditionary Force ashore. Hamstrung by the lack of fighters, FURIOUS continued to operate in the Narvik area until 25th April, when she had to return to Scapa Flow, her turbines damaged by a bomb near-miss.

She was relieved on station by ARK ROYAL and GLORIOUS, the latter rushed home from the Mediterranean Fleet. The two large ships arrived on 24th April, ARK having 28 Skuas and Rocs embarked, and GLORIOUS with 6 Skuas and 18 Sea Gladiators, and they were able to operate nearer to the Army's positions, at that time in the Namsos area.   The fighters began to fly patrols over the army while the Swordfish carried out daily strike and support sorties.   GLORIOUS' principal mission was to fly off 18 Gladiators of 263 Squadron, RAF, to Lake Lesjaskou, after which she returned to Scapa for a fresh load.   The RAF fighters eased the load on the Fleet Air Arm for less than 48 hours, by which time they were all out of action.   ARK ROYAL withdrew on 28th April to replenish, and by this stage the Skuas and Gladiators from the carriers had accounted for nearly 40 enemy aircraft, destroyed and damaged, for the loss of one Skua in combat.

Increased enemy air activity in the Namsos region resulted in ARK ROYAL's operational area being shifted north to the west of Narvik. She returned on 4th May 1940 and provided cover continuously until 24th, by which time GLORIOUS and FURIOUS had brought out more RAF Gladiators and Hurricanes to be based at Bardufoss.   Air support was provided for the amphibious operations around Narvik by the carrier aircraft, as well as strikes on enemy lines of communication and reconnaissance sorties.   Cruiser catapult aircraft were used continuously throughout the campaign for recce and liason, one squadron, 701, performing these duties from a base at Harstadt.   The six Walrus of this unit gave sterling service until the last moment before evacuation and on 6th June the five survivors attacked a German-held harbour prior to embarking in ARK ROYAL for withdrawal on the following day.

ARK had returned at the beginning of June to cover the withdrawal of Allied forces from northern Norway, while GLORIOUS recovered the surviving Gladiators and Hurricanes from Bardufoss.   All landed on board safely, despite the fact that the aircraft were not fitted for deck-landings, but on the following day GLORIOUS was intercepted by SCHARNHORST and GNEISENAU.   Although the two destroyers escorting the carrier attempted to cover her escape by means of a smoke-screen, all three ships were overwhelmed by the heavy gunfire. ACASTA, as she sank, managed to put a torpedo into SCHARNHORST, forcing the battlecruiser to make for Trondheim for emergency repairs.

Five days later, on 13th June 1940, 15 Skuas of 800 and 803 Squadrons were launched from ARK ROYAL to strike at SCHARNHORST at Trondheim.   No surprise was achieved due to the distance the aircraft had to fly over enemy territory from the coast to the target at the head of the fjord.   Eight Skuas were lost to flak and fighters, while the only bomb to hit failed to explode.   As the ship was returning to Germany for full repairs, six Swordfish from Hatston carried out a daylight torpedo attack on her at the extreme limit of their radius of action.   Two aircraft were shot down by the enemy's flak, and no torpedo hits were obtained. After this strike, on 21st June, the ship reached Kiel without further hindrance, but saw no further action until 1941.

Throughout the 1940 Norwegian campaign, Hatston-based Skua squadrons mounted dive-bombing strikes on enemy installations in the Bergen area, achieving notable success against oil fuel storage facilities and shipping for slight losses.   The last blows by the carrier aircraft

DISPOSITION OF VESSELS AND SQUADRONS

FURIOUS

i. **8th to 25th April**
  816 Squadron   9 Swordfish
  818   ,,   9 Swordfish

ii. **May — ferrying**
  804 Squadron   6 Sea Gladiators
  816   ,,   9 Swordfish

iii. **September/October — strikes**
  801 Squadron   9 Skuas
  816   ,,   9 Swordfish
  825   ,,   9 Swordfish

ARK ROYAL — 24th April to 7th June 1940
  800 Squadron   12 Skuas
  801   ,,   6 Skuas & 6 Rocs (to 28th April)
  803   ,,   12 Skuas   (from 30th April)
  810   ,,   12 Swordfish
  820   ,,   12 Swordfish

GLORIOUS — Sunk by gunfire 8th June 1940
  802 Squadron   12 Sea Gladiators
  803   ,,   6 Skuas   (to 28th April)
  804   ,,   6 Sea Gladiators (to 28th April)
  823   ,,   12 Swordfish

---

were struck by 801, 816, and 825 Squadrons from FURIOUS, when the Skuas and Swordfish attacked Trondheim and Tromsø, in September and October. The Tromsø strike saw the first squadron-sized night torpedo attack, nearly a month before Taranto.

ATLANTIC OPERATIONS—THE HOME FLEET AND FORCE H: July 1940 to May 1941

At the end of October 1940, FURIOUS was detached from the Home Fleet for ferrying duties between the United Kingdom and Takoradi, on the Gold Coast, and did not return until the following February. The Home Fleet was therefore without a carrier until the following spring, although FORMIDABLE did join for a few days in December 1940 only to be detached within a week for raider-hunting in the South Atlantic.

ARK ROYAL was sent to Gibraltar immediately after the disastrous SCHARNHORST strike and with HOOD she formed the nucleus of Vice Admiral Somerville's Force H. Force H was brought into being on 28th June 1940, with the dual role of covering the sea areas left unguarded by the immobilisation of the French Navy, and to cover against any westward movement of the Italian Fleet, either into the Western Mediterranean or the Atlantic itself. ARK provided the air component for the attacks on Oran in July 1940, and escorted east-bound Malta convoys, but the main day-to-day employment of Force H

DISPOSITION OF VESSELS AND SQUADRONS

Atlantic — June 1940 to May 1941

FURIOUS — ferrying
801 Squadron	6 Skuas (to end of January 1941)
807 ,,	9 Fulmars (February to April 1941)
825 ,,	9 Swordfish (February to April 1941)

ARGUS — ferrying
825 Squadron	2 Swordfish (detachment only—December to February)
812 ,,	9 Swordfish (April and May 1941)

ARK ROYAL Force H — see under Western Mediterranean

HERMES — left for Indian Ocean in February 1941
814 Squadron	12 Swordfish

FORMIDABLE — December 1940 and January 1941 only — see under Mediterranean Fleet

EAGLE — May to September 1941
813 Squadron	9 Swordfish
824 ,,	9 Swordfish

ALBATROSS — as in previous table

---

was in the Atlantic, searching for surface raiders and blockade runners and guarding against a possible occupation of the Atlantic islands by the Axis.

On Christmas Day, 1940, the heavy cruiser ADMIRAL HIPPER fell in with an important troop convoy which included the carriers FURIOUS and ARGUS, both ferrying RAF aircraft to West Africa. Two Swordfish had been retained in ARGUS for anti-submarine patrols, as well as half a dozen Skuas in FURIOUS. The latter attempted to shadow the enemy while the TSR's were readied for a torpedo strike, but in the event of the inevitable delay HIPPER was driven off by the gunfire of the convoy's cruiser escort.

HERMES and ALBATROSS continued to cover the focal trade areas off West Africa and were joined briefly by FORMIDABLE, searching in the St. Helena area. The damaging of ILLUSTRIOUS on 10th January 1941 in the Mediterranean necessitated a rapid re-deployment of FORMIDABLE. Her departure for the Indian Ocean and the Med. was followed in February by that of HERMES, the smaller ship remaining in the Indian Ocean after operations off Italian Somaliland. ALBATROSS also entered East African waters in 1941, but not until after she had been relieved at Freetown by the belated arrival of the first Royal Air Force maritime patrol aircraft in West Africa, in the late autumn of 1941.

In March 1941 one of ARK ROYAL's Fulmars found and shadowed SCHARNHORST and GNEISENAU in mid-Atlantic, but due to the low visibility and to poor communications, contact was lost before ARK could close the range sufficiently to launch a torpedo strike. The battlecruisers, which were on a raiding cruise, escaped to Brest and Force H spent most of April 1941 in the Atlantic in anticipation of the break-out which did not come finally until February 1942.

The last minutes of COURAGEOUS: torpedoed by U-29 on 17th September 1939 in the South West Approaches   [MoD (Admiralty)]

A Skua and a Gladiator of 801 Squadron at Evanton in the early autumn of 1939, at the time when the Squadron was re-arming with the Skuas
[J. M. Bruen via R. C. Jones]

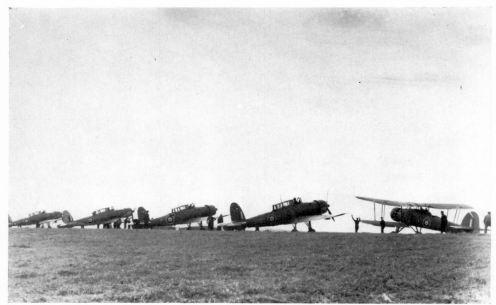

Skuas of 803 Squadron start up prior to a fighter patrol from Hatston during the winter of 1939/40
[IWM

Swordfish 5S of 818 Squadron returns from the third strike on BISMARCK on 27th May 1941 ; the torpedo has been jettisoned and the empty crutches can be seen between the oleos
[IWM

A Fulmar I of VICTORIOUS' 809 Squadron running up prior to launch. The "Donald Duck" motif was a personal rather than a unit marking   [/IWM

A Fulmar I of 809 Squadron is catapulted from VICTORIOUS in Seidisfjord, Iceland. The complex arrangements for raising the aircraft's tail to the flying attitude can be seen to the left of the flight-deck officer   [/IWM

FURIOUS launching 822 Squadron Albacores. She was the only British-built Fleet carrier
with a flush deck and a diminutive island   [IWM

VICTORIOUS in the Arctic 1942: the carrier continues to recover aircraft despite the presence of
an Albacore in the starboard catwalk. 4B of 817 Squadron overshoots with flaps and hook
down while another joins the landing circuit. The ship appears to be going astern, probably
to reduce the wind over the deck   [IWM

FURIOUS making heavy weather of the short Arctic swell—an obvious disadvantage of the open
bow   [IWM

An Albacore of either 817 or 832 Squadron being struck down VIC's after lift   [IWM

October 1943: A Martlet IV of 893 Squadron running-up aft on FORMIDABLE. The wing lashings were held on until the last moment before the aircraft began to taxi as the Martlet's undercarriage track was so narrow, leading to instability in strong winds   [IWM

FORMIDABLE launching Martlet IVs during an Arctic convoy operation. Little natural wind is available, and the steam jet in the bows indicates that what little there is, mainly from the ship's speed, is some 30° off the bow   [IWM

Right: Seafire LIICs in FURIOUS' upper hangar, while Barracuda 5K of 830 Squadron is manhandled on to the lift from the lower hangar

[*IWM*

Below: Early morning 3rd April 1944: EMPEROR, PURSUER, FURIOUS approach the launch position for the first strike on TIRPITZ

[*IWM*

A Barracuda of 830 Squadron is launched from VICTORIOUS while the Corsairs of the top cover (1834 Squadron) form up ahead.   The 1,600lb Armour Piercing bomb can be seen below the Barra's fuselage   [IWM

Barracudas of the second strike (VICTORIOUS' 52 TBR Wing) en route for Kaafjord.   The two aircraft at extreme left and the three at extreme right are carrying 1,600lb AP bombs, while the nearest to the camera is armed with two 600lb A/S bombs   [Crown Copyright

TIRPITZ as the strafing Wildcats of the first strike saw her, with the smoke generators in action
but ineffective   [*IWM*

TIRPITZ at the height of the second attack   [*A. J. Ward (Admiralty)*

SEARCHER'S 898 Squadron returns from the second strike   [*IWM*

Operation "Tungsten"—3rd April 1944: No. 52 TBR Wing returns to VICTORIOUS and begins
the complex folding arrangements required by the Barracuda   [*IWM*

Sub Lieutenant (A) D. J. Frearson of PURSUER's 881 Squadron at the apex of an exaggerated bounce on landing. The Wildcat V's tough undercarriage could absorb a heavy landing such as this whereas most other types would have incurred severe damage   [*D. J. Frearson*

26th April 1944: Barracudas of No. 52 TBR Wing set off on a torpedo strike against a German convoy off Bodo   [*IWM*

Ranging Wildcat Vs aboard PURSUER.   The undersurfaces of the wings of the aircraft to the left show evidence of recent gun-firing   [D. J. Frearson

"M" of 830 Squadron gets airborne for the July strike on TIRPITZ, armed with a 1,600 pounder. The ramp was rigged on FURIOUS' forward flight deck to give the effect of lengthening the old ship's short deck.   Operation "Mascot"—17th July 1944   [IWM

NABOB down by the stern and trailing oil shortly after her damage by torpedo on 22nd August 1944. All but a skeleton ship's company was taken off by the CVE's escorts, and the ship managed to reach Scapa Flow under her own steam   [*IWM*

22nd August 1944—Operation "Goodwood": the Corsairs of 1841 Squadron fly over DEVONSHIRE and TRUMPETER   [*IWM*

The "flagship" of No. 8 TBR Wing overshoots with everything down on return from an A/S patrol (FORMIDABLE 29th August 1944)   [IWM

12th September 1944—Operation "Begonia": TRUMPETER'S Avengers orbit while FURIOUS' Seafires strafe and destroy an M-class minesweeper in Aaramsund   [IWM

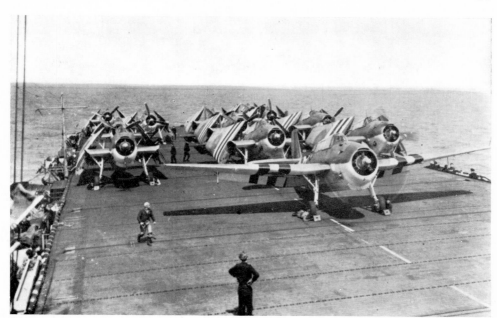

TRUMPETER's 846 Squadron ranged for a minelaying strike in the autumn of 1944   [IWM

27th November 1944: a highly successful strike by IMPLACABLE's Air Group: foreground—
SS KORSNES, centre—RIGEL, and background—SPREE, on fire after attack by Barracudas of
828 Squadron and Fireflies of 1771 Squadron. KORSNES and RIGEL were driven ashore
and lost, while SPREE was severely damaged. Three smaller ships were moderately damaged
                                                                                      [IWM

Deck-park in IMPLACABLE, October 1944. The Firefly is of 1771 Squadron, and the Seafires are of 24 Naval Fighter Wing (P-6N 894, P-5G 887), which was loaned to IMPLACABLE for one series of strikes   [*Admiralty*

One of PUNCHER'S Barracudas bends its hook frame and loses its tail wheel after hitting the aft round-down   [*IWM*

THE HUNT FOR THE BISMARCK

By May 1941 it was known that the new German battleship BISMARCK had completed her sea-trials and was ready at Bergen to sortie into the Atlantic. Final confirmation that she had in fact sailed came late on 22nd May, as the result of a difficult and hazardous reconnaissance sortie by a Fleet Air Arm Maryland of 771 Squadron. The Home Fleet sailed within hours of the report, accompanied by the recently commissioned VICTORIOUS. Until a few hours before the sailing, she had been laden with RAF Hurricanes for Malta and her only aircraft complement consisted of the nine Swordfish of 825 Squadron and six Fulmars of 800Z Squadron. These aircraft were intended only for the defence of the ship during the Mediterranean operation and were unsuited to the strike role, 825 having had little chance for recent torpedo strike practice or training. The Albacores of 828 Squadron were based in the Orkneys at the time, fully worked-up in the strike role, but they came under the operational control of the local AOC Coastal Command and he would not release the squadron in time for embarkation.

BISMARCK was found on 23rd May by the cruisers SUFFOLK and NORFOLK, in the Denmark Strait. The latter used her Walrus for shadowing for nearly forty eight hours, until the enemy was lost again. In the meantime the action between BISMARCK and PRINZ EUGEN on one hand and HOOD and PRINCE OF WALES on the other had been fought, with the loss of HOOD. Some hours later, at around midnight 24th/25th May, the nine Swordfish from VICTORIOUS attacked BISMARCK, which had parted company with PRINZ EUGEN after nightfall on 24th; in spite of the lack of recent torpedo attack training the squadron obtained one hit on the battleship's armoured belt. This was no mean achievement—to score a hit on a fast target, with full powers of manœuvre, in the course of a night bad-weather strike, and all the aircraft returned safely to the carrier. Less fortunate were the Fulmars of 800Z which were used for shadowing to conserve the full strength of the Swordfish strike. Two were lost, the crew of one being rescued by a passing merchant ship. Contact with BISMARCK was lost in bad weather about three hours after the torpedo attack and was not regained for thirty hours.

The Home Fleet searched to the north-west of the last known position of the enemy while Force H was hurriedly moved into the Atlantic to cover a troop convoy to the south-east of the Home Fleet. The BISMARCK was by now running short of fuel, a hit by PRINCE OF WALES having damaged some of her tanks, and the Admiralty anticipated her next move: a run for Brest. Force H, with ARK ROYAL, was moved north to cover such an escape and thus her Swordfish were able to locate and report the enemy only 45 minutes after an RAF Catalina regained contact during the forenoon of 26th May. The RAF aircraft was driven off, damaged, very soon after this first sighting and the Swordfish took over the shadowing until after the first strike by ARK's aircraft. This strike was launched in the early afternoon, some while after the cruiser SHEFFIELD had been detached to maintain close contact. The striking aircrew were not briefed as to the new disposition of the

DISPOSITION OF VESSELS AND SQUADRONS

The BISMARCK Hunt

VICTORIOUS

800Z Squadron	6	Fulmar
825 "	9	Swordfish

ARK ROYAL

807 Squadron	12	Fulmars
808 "	12	Fulmars
810 "	12	Swordfish
818 "	9	Swordfish
820 "	9	Swordfish

---

cruiser, and all 15 Swordfish attacked SHEFFIELD, 11 actually dropping their torpedoes. There was some excuse for the aircrew in that again the attack was mounted in bad weather, low cloud and poor visibility preventing identification after a radar approach. Fortunately all the torpedoes missed, exploded prematurely, or were evaded, and all the aircraft returned safely to ARK.

Armed with the experience of the first abortive attack, 15 Swordfish took off for a second strike just after nightfall. This time there was no mistake; SHEFFIELD directed the strike to the enemy and again the Swordfish carried out an ASV radar assisted attack. Owing to the persistent low cloud and bad visibility, there was no chance for a copybook co-ordinated attack and the aircraft attacked individually. Two hits were obtained; one on the armoured belt did little damage, like that obtained by VICTORIOUS, the other hit right aft and this hit determined the issue, which had been more and more in doubt as BISMARCK headed for Brest at high speed. The steering gear was destroyed, the rudders were jammed, and the propellers damaged. Although her main armament remained intact, BISMARCK was reduced to steaming an unpredictable track. She was harried all night by destroyers which possibly scored further torpedo hits and was finally sunk the following morning by the heavy guns of Force H and the Home Fleet. A third strike of Swordfish witnessed the final battle, and were obliged to jettison their torpedoes unused before returning to ARK ROYAL. The *coup de grace* was given by a torpedo from the cruiser DORSETSHIRE, just 24 hours after firm contact had been regained by the Swordfish.

The heavy cruiser PRINZ EUGEN, which had been detached with engine-room defects, reached Brest safely on 1st June. Aware that she was at large, the carriers VICTORIOUS and ARK ROYAL searched for her and the attendant supply ships. EAGLE, recently transferred from the Mediterranean Fleet, and NELSON covered the area to the west of the Cape Verde Islands, and the carrier aircraft had some degree of success in their searches. On 4th June VICTORIOUS' Swordfish sighted and stopped the supply ship GONZENHEIM, awaiting BISMARCK some 200 miles north of the Azores. Before surface forces could reach the position however the German ship was scuttled. On

6th EAGLE's aircraft found and sank by bombing the U-boat supply ship ELBE, following this up with the detection and surrender of the tanker LOTHRINGEN on 15th June 1941.

As soon as it became certain that PRINZ EUGEN had reached Brest, VICTORIOUS and ARK ROYAL were returned to their normal duties, the two ships joining for a ferry operation in early June, 47 Hurricanes being flown off to Malta on 10th.

THE HOME FLEET IN NORTHERN WATERS: June 1941 to March 1944

With the launching of the German attack on Soviet Russia in June 1941 the Royal Navy, already extended to the limit, was given an additional task—the support of the new ally by both direct and indirect means. A decision was taken at the highest level to strike as early as possible at enemy lines of communication in northern Norway; as part of a co-ordinated operation, carrier aircraft were to strike at Petsamo and Kirkenes, while the minelayer ADVENTURE delivered a large consignment of mines to Archangel.

Accordingly VICTORIOUS and FURIOUS sailed with two cruisers and six destroyers from Scapa, refuelled at Seidisfjord (Iceland) and proceeded to launch their strikes on the afternoon of 30th July 1941. Surprise was lost shortly before the launch when the force was sighted by a shadower, but the operation continued with VICTORIOUS launching 20 Albacores and 9 Fulmars against Kirkenes and FURIOUS launching 9 Albacores, 9 Swordfish, and 6 Fulmars for Petsamo. The

---

DISPOSITION OF VESSELS AND SQUADRONS

Petsamo and Kirkenes
VICTORIOUS
809 Squadron	12 Fulmars
827 „	12 Albacores
828 „	9 Albacores

FURIOUS
800 Squadron	9 Fulmars
880A Flight	4 Sea Hurricanes
812 Squadron	9 Swordfish
817 „	9 Albacores

Home Fleet — August 1941 to December 1942
VICTORIOUS
809 Squadron	12 Fulmars
802B Flight	2 Martlet IIIs (September 1941 only)
817 Squadron	9 Albacores
832 „	12 Albacores
820 „	12 Albacores (in place of 832 Sqn November 1941 to February 1942)

ARGUS — ferrying
802B Flight	2 Martlet IIIs (August and September 1941)

AVENGER
802 Squadron	6 Sea Hurricanes
883 „	6 Sea Hurricanes
825 Flight	3 Swordfish

(6 spare Sea Hurricanes embarked)

air defence of the force rested with 4 Sea Hurricanes from FURIOUS and the 3 remaining Fulmars aboard VICTORIOUS.

The enemy were ready for the strike on Kirkenes. What little shipping there was in the harbour was under way and the defences were fully alerted. The Albacores sank one 2,000ton freighter, set another on fire, and caused minor damage ashore, but the fighters and the flak destroyed 11 of their number and of the survivors only one was undamaged. The Fulmars destroyed two Bf 110s and a Bf 109, losing two of their own number to Bf 109s, by which they were totally outclassed; the undamaged Albacore destroyed a Ju 87 with its single front gun.

Opposition was less intense at Petsamo, but there were few targets. One small steamer was sunk and some wooden jetties destroyed by torpedoes, for the loss of an Albacore and two Fulmars.

After recovering the surviving aircraft, the force withdrew unscathed, the Sea Hurricanes shooting down a shadower on 31st July. FURIOUS returned to Scapa short of fuel after transferring Albacores to VICTORIOUS to make good the losses in the latter's air group. A few armed reconnaissance sorties were flown during the next few days, but they enjoyed no success and no further strikes were launched.

Late in August 1941 the first North Russian convoy left for Archangel. Covered by the Home Fleet, the convoy included ARGUS which was ferrying 24 RAF Hurricanes in addition to the two Martlet IIIs embarked for her own protection. The remainder of the Hurricane Wing, No. 151, was crated in merchant ships in the convoy. After a safe arrival at Murmansk, whence the Hurricanes were to operate, the Martlets were transferred to VICTORIOUS, which proceeded with the Home Fleet to strike at enemy shipping in the Bodø area. On this occasion the strike incurred no losses while the Albacores sank two merchant ships and damaged an aluminium works in Glomfjord. This strike, on 12th September, was followed in October by another raid in the same area. On 9th, Albacores damaged a total of 13,000 gross register tons of enemy-controlled merchant shipping; all the strike aircraft returned safely to the carrier, although two were destroyed in landing accidents after flak damage.

These operations were the last undertaken by VICTORIOUS' aircraft against Norwegian coastal shipping targets for more than two years, although she continued to serve with the Home Fleet until July 1942, taking part in most of the covering operations for the Arctic convoys. The only attack was against TIRPITZ on 9th March 1942. The torpedo strike failed by a narrow margin, one torpedo passing within 30 feet of the battleship's stern; too few aircraft, twelve, were involved and the leader of the strike had insufficient recent experience of this difficult form of attack for any real hope of success. Two aircraft were shot down by the flak.

The effect of this attack upon the German High Command was far-reaching. While the C-in-C Home Fleet was not impressed with the results, the enemy realized that TIRPITZ had only narrowly escaped the fate of her sister-ship BISMARCK. Hitler himself laid down that TIRPITZ was not to remain at sea if it was known that a carrier was at sea with the Home Fleet. The practical result of this policy as far as the Royal Navy was concerned was that the battleship was never again attacked by aircraft on the high seas. TIRPITZ did sail against PQ 17, the last Arctic convoy to be covered by VICTORIOUS, but as soon as it was known that the carrier was at sea she was ordered to return to her fjord. Although the threat of her intervention led to the disastrous "scatter" order to the convoy, she took no part in the decimation of the unprotected merchant ships.

The largest share of the destruction was inflicted by air attack; 14 of the 22 ships lost were sunk by the well-drilled torpedo-bombers, which might have achieved less success if they had been opposed by the considerable volume of AA fire available to a strongly escorted convoy in good order. It was realized that in future close aircraft carrier escort would have to be provided for these convoys if the losses were to be kept within acceptable limits. The U-boats were not at this stage the menace they were in the Atlantic, the extreme weather conditions making life just as difficult for the submarines as for the surface vessels.

The sailing of PQ 18, the next in the series of eastbound convoys, was delayed until September 1942. The delay was imposed by two considerations. The "Pedestal" convoy to Malta was run in August 1942 and all available carriers were committed to the operation. Secondly, the passage of the two months meant that the Arctic nights were longer, giving the Lufwaffe less time to find the convoys and to mount the attacks. AVENGER, the second of the American-built escort carriers, was earmarked for the provision of fighter cover for the convoy and the delay gave her time to complete the work-up and for her fighter squadrons to absorb the lessons learnt in the Mediterranean convoy air battle.

When AVENGER joined PQ 18 off Iceland on 9th September 1942 she had 12 Sea Hurricanes and 3 Swordfish embarked, with another half-dozen fighters dismantled in the hangar as a first-line reserve. For the three days after 12th September these few aircraft fought a series of vicious actions against Luftflotte V as the enemy attempted to repeat their success. On 12th the first massed torpedo strike sank eight merchant ships, with the fighters drawn out of position. Thereafter the Sea Hurricanes looked after their charges so well that no other ship was sunk by air attack until the portion of the convoy proceeding to Archangel had left the aircraft carrier's immediate protection. Attacks on 13th and 14th September were broken up by the Sea Hurricanes, denying the enemy the set-piece formation vital to the success of the German tactics. The fighters engaged in 30 combats, in the course of which they destroyed five Ju 88s and He 111s, and damaged another 21. Only in four of the combats was no claim made; the low proportions of victories was largely attributable to the inadequate armament of the Sea Hurricane IB, which did not allow sufficient weight of fire to be delivered in the limited time available in each firing pass. Altogether 41 enemy aircraft failed to return, according to German records. Four Sea Hurricanes were lost, three at one time to the undisciplined AA. fire of the merchant ships, which compounded their irresponsibility by opening fire from time to time on returning Swordfish. Three of the naval fighter pilots were rescued by the escort, the only fatality being a pilot shot down by the return fire of an enemy formation.

U-boats sank only three ships from the convoy and they lost U-589, sunk by destroyers after a position report by one of the Swordfish. Two merchant ships were sunk in the White Sea by torpedo aircraft after AVENGER had entered the Kola Inlet. During the attack, on 18th September, the Sea Hurricane IA from the catapult-armed merchant ship EMPIRE MORN destroyed two He 115 torpedo bombers and saved the convoy from further damage.

After their crippling losses the Luftwaffe were never again able to mount air attacks on the North Russian convoys on the scale encountered by PQ 17 and PQ 18 in June and September 1942. Subsequent torpedo attacks were made in smaller numbers and the participating crews never displayed the same high degree of skill. The U-boat became the main enemy but thanks to the provision of adequate, well-trained anti-submarine carrier squadrons they never attained the same rate of sinkings as their North Atlantic counterparts.

The Arctic convoys were redesignated after PQ 18—JW eastbound and RA westbound, but owing to the needs of the Fleet for the invasion of North Africa in November 1942, no further escort carriers were available until February 1943, when DASHER joined JW 53 but was forced to return with weather damage after only two days with the convoy, which suffered no losses.

DISPOSITION OF VESSELS AND SQUADRONS

Home Fleet — 1943
FURIOUS — from end of February 1943
801 Squadron	9	Seafires	
822 ,,	9	Albacores	(to end of June 1943)
825 ,,	9	Swordfish	(plus 6 Sea Hurricanes from July 1943)
881 ,,	6	Martlet IVs	(July 1943 only)
827 ,,	12	Barracudas	(from October 1943)
830 ,,	9	Barracudas	(from October 1943)

DASHER — lost in aviation gasoline explosion 27th March 1943
891 Squadron	9	Sea Hurricanes
816 ,,	6	Swordfish

ILLUSTRIOUS — June to August 1943
878 Squadron	12	Martlet IVs
890 ,,	8	Martlet IVs
894 ,,	9	Seafires
810 ,,	12	Barracudas

UNICORN — July 1943 only
887 Squadron	10	Seafires
818 ,,	4	Swordfish
824 ,,	9	Swordfish

USS RANGER — September and October 1943
Fighting Squadron (VF-) 41	27 F4F-4	(Wildcat)
Bombing Squadron (VF-) 41	27 SBD-5	(Dauntless)
Torpedo Squadron (VT-) 41	18 TBF-1	(Avenger)

Throughout 1943 Home Fleet carrier operations were circumscribed by the lack of suitable ships. FURIOUS was with the Fleet for most of the year, but her small complement and limited endurance precluded sustained flying off an enemy coast; the majority of the Fleet carriers were occupied in the Mediterranean and the Pacific, while from July 1943 INDOMITABLE was repairing heavy torpedo damage. The North Atlantic convoy routes had greater priority for escorts and escort carriers (CVEs) than the Arctic, and thus no carrier sailed as close escort with a JW/RA convoy until February 1944, by which time sufficient numbers of the smaller ships had become available, together with more suitable aircraft types. The Home Fleet normally took the Fleet carrier to sea when covering the convoys, FORMIDABLE relieving FURIOUS in October 1943 to cover a couple of these operations.

There were only three operations of an offensive nature by the Home Fleet carriers during 1943. Two of these took place in July, as part of a diversionary sweep to draw off attention from the Allied landings in Sicily. FURIOUS took part in the first, and ILLUSTRIOUS and UNICORN in the second; the only positive results took the form of the destruction of five Bv 138 shadowers at the hands of the carriers' Martlet IVs. There was no obvious enemy reaction to the sweeps.

The third operation marked the only strike mounted by the United States Navy in northern European waters. The carrier RANGER was lent to the Home Fleet for a short while in the late autumn of 1943 to replace ILLUSTRIOUS, redeployed to the Mediterranean. RANGER's Air Group 41 struck at Bodø on 4th October 1943 and the Dauntlesses and Avengers sank five enemy ships of 27,000grt, and damaged another 5 ships of 19,000grt for the loss of only five American aircraft to flak. The Germans had been lulled into a false sense of security as a result of the lack of offensive carrier action over the preceding two years, and the anchorage and harbour was full of shipping when the strike was delivered, a situation never repeated during the ensuing eighteen months of Fleet Air Arm strikes.

THE STRIKES ON THE TIRPITZ: April to August 1944

Despite the presence of a strong surface squadron in Norwegian waters throughout 1943, the German Navy was used in a most circumspect fashion. TIRPITZ and SCHARNHORST bombarded Spitzbergen on 6th September, doing little real damage. Later in the month TIRPITZ was severely damaged by midget submarines at her anchorage in Kaafjord, the Admiralty estimating that the damage would take at least six months to repair. SCHARNHORST was destroyed by DUKE OF YORK on Boxing Day 1943 while attempting to intercept a convoy; the Battle of the North Cape was the last encounter between capital ships on the high seas.

The Fleet Air Arm squadrons had been re-armed and trained to a high standard of efficiency during 1943. The first evidence of just how thorough this training had been came in the course of a strike on TIRPITZ in April 1944.

DISPOSITION OF VESSELS AND SQUADRONS

Operation "Tungsten" — the TIRPITZ Strike on 3rd April 1944

VICTORIOUS
1834 Squadron	14 Corsairs	
1836 „	14 Corsairs	
827 „	12 Barracudas	(No. 8 TBR Wing)
829 „	9 Barracudas	(No. 52 TBR Wing)

FURIOUS
801 Squadron	9 Seafires	
880 „	9 Seafires	
830 „	9 Barracudas	(No. 8 TBR Wing)
831 „	12 Barracudas	(No. 52 TBR Wing)

EMPEROR
800 Squadron	10 Hellcats
804 „	10 Hellcats

PURSUER
881 Squadron	10 Wildcat V
896 „	10 Wildcat V

SEARCHER
882 Squadron	10 Wildcat V
898 „	10 Wildcat V

FENCER — A/S CVE
842 Squadron	12 Swordfish II & 8 Wildcat IV

Further Strikes on the TIRPITZ

Operation "Mascot" — 17th July 1944:

FORMIDABLE
1841 Squadron	18 Corsairs
827 „	12 Barracudas
830 „	12 Barracudas

FURIOUS
880 Squadron	12 Seafires
1840 „	20 Hellcats
842 Flight	3 Swordfish

INDEFATIGABLE
894 Squadron	16 Seafires
1770 „	12 Fireflies
820 „	12 Barracudas
826 „	12 Barracudas

Operation "Goodwood" — 22nd-29th August 1944:

FORMIDABLE
1841 Squadron	18 Corsairs
1842 „	12 Corsairs
826 „	12 Barracudas
828 „	12 Barracudas

FURIOUS
801 Squadron	12 Seafires
880 „	12 Seafires
827 „	12 Barracudas

INDEFATIGABLE
887 Squadron	16 Seafires
894 „	16 Seafires
1840 „	12 Hellcats
1770 „	12 Fireflies
1770 „	12 Fireflies
820 „	12 Barracudas

NABOB — A/S CVE — torpedoed by U-354 on 22nd August 1944
852 Squadron	12 Avengers & 4 Wildcats

TRUMPETER
846 Squadron	8 Avengers & 4 Wildcats

Fully aware that TIRPITZ would soon be ready for sea after the damage inflicted by the midget submarine attack had been made good, the Commander-in-Chief of the Home Fleet planned and executed Operation "Tungsten"—a carrier strike on the battleship at her anchorage. "Tungsten" was probably the most carefully planned, briefed, and rehearsed strike undertaken by the Fleet Air Arm during the War. A dummy range was built on Loch Erriboll in Caithness and the Barracudas of No. 8 Torpedo Bomber Reconnaissance Wing and No. 52 TBR Wing, from FURIOUS and VICTORIOUS respectively, rehearsed the attack with their supporting fighters, the last occasion being on 28th March 1944, less than a week before the strike itself.

The Home Fleet's Second Battle Squadron sailed for the operation on 30th, under the command of Sir Henry Moore, with the C-in-C Home Fleet, Admiral Sir Bruce Fraser in DUKE OF YORK. ANSON, SHEFFIELD, JAMAICA, and ROYALIST (flag Rear Admiral, Escort Carriers, Rear Admiral A. W. La T. Bisset) made up the heavy cover, while the carrier squadron comprised VICTORIOUS, FURIOUS, EMPEROR, SEARCHER, PURSUER and FENCER, the whole screened by 12 destroyers. Air A/S support was provided by FENCER, while her Wildcats and FURIOUS' Seafires were to provide the Fleet air defence during the strike. In order that the Wings which had rehearsed together should strike together, the Fleet carriers exchanged a Barracuda squadron apiece before the force sailed.

FURIOUS and the escort carriers headed for the launch position direct, while the battleships and VICTORIOUS provided distant heavy cover for the Northern Russian convoy JW 58. The re-united force reached the flying-off position, 120 miles north-west of Kaafjord, in the early hours of 3rd April 1944 and at 0430 No. 8 TBR Wing was launched from the Fleet carriers, with an escort of about 40 Corsairs, Hellcats and Wildcats. The strike reached the target about an hour later, as TIRPITZ was getting underway for the first time since her damaging. The coordinated attack was entirely successful, with the Barracudas enjoying complete surprise, and considerable damage was inflicted. An hour later the 19 Barracudas of No. 52 TBR Wing attacked, adding further damage. 14 direct hits were obtained by the 40 dive-bombers, and in addition to the extensive damage to the superstructure and fire-control systems, casualties aboard TIRPITZ amounted to 438 killed or wounded. A supply ship, C. A. LARSEN, was severely damaged by bombs, and two other enemy ships damaged to a lesser extent.

Two Barracudas were lost during the strikes, one from each attack, another was lost on take-off, while a Hellcat was forced to ditch alongside a destroyer. The slight losses to flak were undoubtedly due to the efficient support given by the straffing Hellcats and Wildcats, which put the target's flak directors out of action and shot up the flak positions ashore immediately before the dive bombers entered their dives. This flak suppression role became more and more the prime employment of the carrier fighters in subsequent operations off the Norwegian coast, in the absence of strong enemy fighter opposition.

The damage to TIRPITZ put her out of action for three months, reducing the anxiety felt as to the safety of the Arctic convoys and releasing many modern warships for service in other theatres of war.

The proficiency of the young aircrew was significant. Not since the strike on the Italian battlefleet at Taranto in November 1940 had the results of a carefully planned attack been so gratifying. In place of 20 Swordfish, crewed by 40 experienced aircrew, there were 121 Barracudas, Corsairs, Hellcats and Wildcats and of the 163 aircrew involved no less than 138 were Reserve aircrew from six countries, most seeing combat for the first time.

Further strikes by aircraft from FURIOUS, FORMIDABLE and INDEFATIGABLE were undertaken in July and August 1944. A total of five strikes attacked on four separate days, but the degree of surprise achieved by the April strike was never repeated. The main defence lay in the use of smoke screens to blanket the entire anchorage and the Barracudas were forced to bomb blind on every occasion. As a result, only on 24th August did the bombers manage to obtain hits. Of the two hits one penetrated the main armoured belt, the only naval bomb to do so, but it failed to explode.

No enemy air opposition was encountered during the strikes on TIRPITZ, and apart from the aircraft losses to flak and other operational causes, the only naval unit to become a casualty was the Canadian-manned escort carrier NABOB. She was torpedoed off the North Cape on 22nd August by U-354 but despite a hole 11 yards square below the waterline aft she managed to reach Scapa Flow under her own steam, even managing to fly off an anti-submarine patrol of two Avengers during the following night, recovering both although the ship was well down by the stern. Appropriately U-354 was sunk by Swordfish from VINDEX only three days later, off Bear Island; NABOB was assessed as being beyond economical repair and was scrapped at the end of the War.

TIRPITZ was finally sunk at Tromsø on 12th November 1944 by Royal Air Force Lancasters, using 12,000lb "Tallboy" bombs. Her entire career had been circumscribed by the tremendous respect held by the German High Command for the Home Fleet's aircraft carriers. Her sister-ship had been sunk only because ARK ROYAL's Swordfish had been able to disable her in mid-Atlantic, and TIRPITZ herself had had a narrow escape from the Albacores of VICTORIOUS in March 1942. On the other hand, the threat imposed by her presence in Norwegian waters tied down the same carriers, as well as capital ships and cruisers of both the Royal and United States Navies, all of which were urgently required elsewhere.

OPERATIONS IN NORWEGIAN COASTAL WATERS:
April 1944 to May 1945

Between 26th April 1944 and 8th May 1945, aircraft from Fleet and escort carriers undertook more than 30 operations off the Norwegian coast and against coastal targets, in addition to the strikes on TIRPITZ.

DISPOSITION OF VESSELS AND SQUADRONS

Carrier Strikes in Norwegian Waters 1944

FURIOUS — 11 operations between April 1944 and September 1944. Aircraft complement varied, but largely as for last series of TIRPITZ strikes.

VICTORIOUS — 2 anti-shipping strikes in April and June 1944. Aircraft complement as in Operation "Tungsten"

INDEFATIGABLE — 2 anti-shipping operations in August 1944. Complement as in Operation "Goodwood".

IMPLACABLE — 6 days of operations between late October and early December 1944

887 Squadron	16 Seafires	(October)	
894 ,,	16 Seafires	(October)	
801 ,,	12 Seafires	(from December)	
880 ,,	12 Seafires	(from November)	
828 ,,	12 Barracudas	(21 after November)	
841 ,,	9 Barracudas	(amalgamated with 828 in November)	
1771 ,,	12 Fireflies		

Escort Carriers in Home Fleet Strikes — 1944 and 1945

CAMPANIA — 2 operations — October and January 1944-45

813 Squadron	12 Swordfish & 4 Wildcats (October)
813 ,,	8 Swordfish & 8 Wildcats (January 1945)
842 ,,	4 Wildcats (Fighter Flight lent from FENCER)

EMPEROR — 2 strikes — May 1944

800 Squadron	10 Hellcats
804 ,,	10 Hellcats

FENCER — 3 strikes — June and October 1944

842 Squadron	8 Wildcats (June)
881 ,,	10 Wildcats (June)
842 ,,	4 Wildcats (October)
852 ,,	4 Avengers & 4 Wildcats (October)

NAIRANA — 1 operation in January 1945

835 Squadron	14 Swordfish & 6 Wildcats

NABOB — 1 minelaying operation in August 1944 — Complement as "Goodwood"

PREMIER — 9 operations between November 1944 and March 1945

856 Squadron	12 Avengers (to January 1945)
846 ,,	4 Avengers (December 1944)
856 ,,	8 Avengers and 8 Wildcats (4 Wildcats ex-881 Sqn)
881 ,,	12 Wildcats (February 1945)
856 ,,	7 Avengers (February 1945)

(note: the complement after February 1945 was 8 Avengers and 8 Wildcats of 856 Squadron. The frequent exchange and reshuffling of aircraft was a feature of CVE operation in the Home Fleet at this time.)

PURSUER — one operation in April 1944 and 3 in November 1944

881 Squadron	10 Wildcats (April 1944)
896 ,,	10 Wildcats (April 1944)
881 ,,	20 Wildcats (November 1944)

PUNCHER — 3 operations between February and April 1945

821 Squadron	10 Barracudas and 8 Wildcats

QUEEN — 4 operations between March and May 1945

853 Squadron	12 Avengers & 4 Wildcats

SEARCHER — i. 3 operations in April & May 1944; ii. 4 operations March to May 1945

i—882 Squadron	10 Wildcats
i—898 ,,	10 Wildcats
ii—882 ,,	20 Wildcats
ii—746A Flight	2 Fireflies

STRIKER — 4 operations — April, May, & June 1944

824 Squadron	12 Swordfish & 6 Sea Hurricanes (April)
824 ,,	12 Swordfish (May)
898 ,,	10 Wildcats (May)
824 ,,	12 Swordfish & 10 Wildcats (June)

DISPOSITION—continued

TRUMPETER — 13 operations — August 1944 to May 1945, plus an Arctic
convoy operation in March 1945

846 Squadron	12	Avengers & 4 Wildcats (August)
846 ,,	12	Avengers (September)
852 ,,	6	Avengers (September)
846 ,,	8	Avengers & 4 Wildcats (October)
852 ,,	8	Avengers (October)
881 ,,	20	Wildcats (December)
846 ,,	8	Avengers & 8 Wildcats (from January 1945)
881 ,,	4	Wildcats (January 1945 only)

Enemy coast-wise shipping was attacked with bomb, rocket, gun and mine; factories and port installations, depots and airfields were straffed and bombed; fighter cover was provided for surface forces interdicting enemy convoys and in June 1944 further diversionary sweeps were made against southern Norway, to simulate pre- invasion reconnaissance, while the Allies landed in Normandy. The naval aircraft ranged between Narvik in the north and Stavanger in the south, the striking forces numbering anything between 12 and 50 fighters and bombers or mine-layers.

The planning of shipping strikes in the Leads, an almost continuous chain of islands off the west coast of Norway, required accurate, up-to-date intelligence while the strikes themselves needed perfect timing and complete surprise to succeed. The Leads and the indented coastline afforded excellent cover for shipping in all but the most ideal weather conditions and there were numerous protected anchorages, well-supplied with flak of all calibres. Few Luftwaffe fighters were encountered and when they did attempt to interfere the escorting Hellcats and Wildcats looked after their charges so well that no Barracuda or Avenger was lost in air combat while on a strike—a far cry from the experience at Kirkenes in July 1941.

Four Fleet carriers saw action off Norway during the period April to December 1944. With their larger aircraft complements and better planning, briefing and arming facilities, the Fleet carriers inflicted the majority of the actual damage, destroying and seriously damaging nearly 100,000 gross register tons of enemy-controlled merchant shipping, in addition to the damage inflicted on TIRPITZ and other smaller warships. FURIOUS took part in the greatest number of operations, 11 in addition to seven strikes on TIRPITZ and three strikes which were cancelled at a late stage because of unfavourable weather. Between April and September 1944, her experienced No. 8 Torpedo Bomber Reconnaissance Wing destroyed and contributed to the destruction of over 25,000grt and to the damaging of another 21,000grt. Launched in 1916, FURIOUS wore herself out in these continuous operations and was withdrawn from service in September 1944.

VICTORIOUS and INDEFATIGABLE participated in two operations apiece, the former attacking shipping with FURIOUS, and the latter providing fighter cover for minelaying by Avengers from escort carriers. IMPLACABLE was the last Fleet carrier to serve with the Home Fleet during World War II, seeing her first action between October and December 1944. In a series of strikes her aircraft destroyed and damaged nearly 40,000grt of enemy coastal shipping, as well as driving ashore U-1060, later to be completely destroyed by RAF bombing. The size of the ships used for enemy coastal supply was relatively small, and the tonnage sunk and damaged was correspondingly low although the numbers of ships sunk continued high. Until the departure of the Fleet carriers for the Pacific at the end of 1944, the Fleet Air Arm caused more damage to enemy shipping off Norway than any other offensive arm.

It was the escort carriers however which bore the brunt of the Fleet Air Arm offensive in the north. All the coastal minelaying by the naval aircraft was carried out from these ships, as well as the shipping strikes mounted on similar lines to those executed by the Fleet carriers. The Grumman/General Motors Avenger was the primary strike aircraft; only one carrier, PUNCHER, employed Barracudas. Fighter cover, escort and support, was provided in the main by Wildcats, although EMPEROR operated Hellcats and STRIKER still had Sea Hurricanes embarked in the autumn of 1944. The General Motors' Wildcat V and VI showed itself to be an excellent fighter, despite the relatively low performance. On the two occasions when Wildcats were called upon to defend Avenger strikes, they came away without loss, destroying and damaging five superior Bf 109Gs on the second occasion, on 26th March 1945.

The minelaying and bombing severely disrupted the enemy's lines of communication with his garrison troops in Norway, which depended upon the free use of the coastal waterways. More manpower and material had to be devoted to the protection of these seaways than Germany could well afford at this late stage of the War. As well as the anti-shipping operations, the Fleet Air Arm fighters worked over shore targets, as previously mentioned. In straffing attacks on airfields, as well as in the rare air combat, they destroyed about 40 enemy aircraft, ranging from the only Fw 190A to be shot down by a Hellcat, to the Bv 222V2 straffed and set on fire at Sørveisen by the Fireflies of 1771 Squadron.

Aircraft carrier complements varied considerably in the Escort Carrier Squadron, where a policy of "horses for courses" was adopted—certain squadrons specialising in certain roles. The operations were too many to enumerate individually, but two are worthy of particular note.

On 28th January 1945, Swordfish of CAMPANIA's 813 Squadron carried out a night shipping strike on Vaagsö. The only shipping there was trawlers, and three of these were sunk in the moonlight augmented by flares, with A/S rockets. This was the only night strike by an escort carrier group, PREMIER and NAIRANA flying covering sorties, and the lack of success was typical of the difficulties encountered in finding suitable targets in these waters.

The final Fleet Air Arm strike of the European War was a brilliantly executed attack on a U-boat depot ship at Kilbotn, near Harstad. In a carefully planned and co-ordinated strike, 44 Avengers and Wildcats from QUEEN, TRUMPETER and SEARCHER sank the 5,000ton depot ship BLACK WATCH, U-711 alongside, and an 860grt merchant ship. TRUMPETER'S experienced 846 Squadron was responsible for the sinking of the depot ship and U-boat, while QUEEN's 853 sank the m/v. Flak suppression by the Wildcats of all three CVEs was so effective that only one aircraft of each type was lost, in spite of intense ground-fire. After this operation, on 4th May, the force moved south to cover the Allied occupation of Denmark, where fighter and A/S patrols were provided until 8th May 1954.

The CVEs suffered from lack of speed and space, the former resulting in their being hard pressed to make a given flying-off position to enable their aircraft to intercept and attack enemy shipping found by earlier reconnaissance. In all, 12 escort carriers were employed at various periods with the Home Fleet for offensive operations—TRUMPETER seeing most service. She participated in 13 operations between August 1944 and May 1945, in addition to a round voyage with an Arctic convoy in March 1945.

Although their disadvantages hampered the full and effective use of the escort carriers with the Home Fleet, they served a vital function. The enemy was kept fully aware of the vulnerability of his long seaward flank, distracting his attention from the valuable Arctic convoys which delivered more and more war supplies to the advancing Russians. The mining campaign tied down many small craft which had to keep the channels clear.

ESCORT CARRIERS WITH NORTH RUSSIAN CONVOYS:
February 1944 to May 1945

After the passage of PQ 18 and the returning QP 14 in September 1942, the convoys were re-designated, mainly for security reasons. Eastbound convoys were pre-fixed JW, beginning with JW 51A in December 1942, while the westbound convoys had the RA prefix.

Although DASHER made a brief excursion with JW 53 in February 1943, the first escort carrier to complete the round voyage, CHASER, did not sail until February 1944, joining the close escort of JW/RA 57. Although the trade protection carrier manning situation did not allow of an earlier deployment, the Arctic route was of a lower priority than the Atlantic, where the available CVEs had seen all their service in 1943.

The re-appearance of the escort carrier on the Arctic scene was dramatic. CHASER's 816 Squadron, a composite unit, sank two U-boats and shared a third on successive days in early March 1944, while escorting the returning convoy RA 57. The next convoy operation, for which two CVEs were provided, saw the destruction of another two U-boats, one shared, and the serious damaging of three more. Fighters from ACTIVITY and TRACKER foiled an attempt at a set-piece U-boat trap by disposing of six enemy shadowers in two days, thus depriving the Captain, U-boats, Norway, of accurate position reports of the convoy,

DISPOSITION OF VESSELS AND SQUADRONS

Escort Carriers with the Arctic Convoys — February 1944 to May 1945

JW & RA 57 — February & March 1944
  CHASER   — 816 Squadron   11 Swordfish & 11 Wildcats
Kills: U-366, U-973. Shared: U-472, with ONSLAUGHT

JW & RA 58 — March & April 1944
  ACTIVITY   — 819 Squadron   3 Swordfish & 7 Wildcats
  TRACKER   — 846 Squadron   12 Avengers & 7 Wildcats
Kills: U-288. Shared: U-355, with BEAGLE. Damaged: U-362, U-673, U-990.
Enemy aircraft destroyed: 3 Fw 200C, 2 Ju 88, 1 Bv 138C

RA 59 — May 1944
  ACTIVITY   — 819 Squadron   3 Swordfish & 7 Wildcats
  FENCER   — 842 Squadron   11 Swordfish & 9 Wildcats
Kills: U-277, U-674, U-959. Enemy aircraft destroyed: 1 Bv 138C.

JW 59 & RA 59A — August 1944
  VINDEX   — 825 Squadron   12 Swordfish & 6 Sea Hurricanes
  STRIKER   — 824 Squadron   12 Swordfish & 10 Wildcats
Kill: U-354. Shared: U-344, U-394, with MERMAID and Others.
Enemy aircraft destroyed: 3 Bv 138C

JW & RA 60 — September 1944
  CAMPANIA   — 813 Squadron   12 Swordfish & 4 Wildcats
  STRIKER   — 824   „   12 Swordfish & 10 Wildcats
Kill: U-921

JW & RA 61 — October & November 1944
  VINDEX   — 811 Squadron   12 Swordfish & 4 Wildcats
  TRACKER   — 853   „   10 Avengers & 6 Wildcats
  NAIRANA   — 835   „   14 Swordfish & 6 Wildcats
No Kills — no convoy losses

JW & RA 61A (2 Liners carrying returning Russian POWs) — November 1944
  CAMPANIA   — 813 Squadron   12 Swordfish & 4 Wildcats
Enemy aircraft destroyed: 2 Bv 138C

JW & RA 62 — December 1944
  CAMPANIA   — 813 Squadron   12 Swordfish & 4 Wildcats
  NAIRANA   — 835   „   14 Swordfish & 6 Wildcats
Kill U-365. Enemy aircraft destroyed: 2 Ju 88 (torpedo bombers) & 1 Bv 138C

JW & RA 63 — January 1945
  VINDEX   — 825 Squadron   12 Swordfish & 7 Wildcats
No Kills — no ships in convoy lost

JW & RA 64 — February 1945
  CAMPANIA   — 813 Squadron   12 Swordfish, 4 Wildcats, & 1 NF Fulmar
  NAIRANA   — 835   „   14 Swordfish & 6 Wildcats
Enemy aircraft destroyed: 4 Ju 88 (torpedo bombers) plus 5 probables

JW & RA 65 — March 1945
  CAMPANIA   — 813 Squadron   12 Swordfish & 7 Wildcats
  TRUMPETER — 846   „   8 Avengers & 8 Wildcats
No Kills — 2 ships lost in the Kola Inlet

JW & RA 66 — April 1945
  VINDEX   — 813 Squadron   8 Swordfish & 12 Wildcats
  PREMIER   — 856   „   12 Avengers
One Kill by surface escorts — none by aircraft

JW & RA 67 — May 1945 (This convoy sailed 4 days after VE-Day but the
                           escort was maintained at full strength as the attitude
                           of the U-boat commanders was unknown. The
                           convoy was not molested.)
  QUEEN   — 853 Squadron   8 Avengers & 8 Wildcats

needed to achieve concentration. The sailing of this convoy, JW 58, was coincident with the "Tungsten" strike on the battleship TIRPITZ: with six carriers in that force, the Royal Navy possessed eight carriers in Arctic waters, with 190 aircraft embarked. Only four years before there had been only FURIOUS with 18 Swordfish, no fighters and no radar.

After JW/RA 58, seven U-boats were sunk in three convoy operations; three were sunk in a 48-hour period at the beginning of May 1944, by the unaided efforts of FENCER's Swordfish. Four more shadowers were destroyed during this period, and of 304 merchant ships sailing in these nine JW/RA convoys only four were sunk by enemy action. Although carrier escort was provided for the remaining seven round convoys, only one more U-boat was sunk, by CAMPANIA, in December 1944. The U-boats, after their mauling at the hands of the carrier aircraft, were fitted with Schnorkel equipment and preferred to hunt in coastal waters where the Russians were responsible for counter-measures. Only four more merchant ships were sunk by U-boat attack on Arctic convoys during 1945.

DISPOSITION OF VESSELS AND SQUADRONS

The Trade Protection War — Fighter Catapult Ships

PEGASUS	807 Squadron —	3 Fulmars; 9 convoys covered between December 1940 and July 1941
PATIA		Sunk in April 1941, before embarking her aircraft
SPRINGBANK	804 Squadron —	1 Fulmar; over 5 convoys between May & September 1941
ARIGVANI	804 Squadron —	1 Fulmar (May to August 1941) 1 Sea Hurricane (August to October 1941) Ship damaged by U-boat in October 1941 while with 11th convoy
MAPLIN	804 Squadron —	1 Sea Hurricane, increasing to 3 in late 1941 over 8 convoys between June 1941 and June 1942 1 Fw 200C destroyed on 3rd August 1941

(SPRINGBANK was sunk on 27th September 1941 while escorting a Gibraltar convoy

Catapult Armed Merchant ships (Royal Air Force aircraft and pilot)

CAM ships lost	CAM ships using their aircraft in anger	other CAM ships
MICHAEL E	EMPIRE LAWRENCE	EMPIRE DAY
EMPIRE RAINBOW	(lost)	EMPIRE FAITH
EMPIRE HUDSON	EMPIRE HEATH	EMPIRE EVE
EMPIRE DELL	EMPIRE DARWIN	EMPIRE FLAME
EMPIRE OCEAN	EMPIRE MOON	EMPIRE CLIVE
EMPIRE SHACKLETON	EMPIRE FOAM	EMPIRE FRANKLIN
EMPIRE SPRING	EMPIRE TIDE	EMPIRE GALE
EMPIRE BURTON	EMPIRE MORN	EMPIRE RAY
EMPIRE WAVE	(2 launches)	EMPIRE ROWAN
EMPIRE SUM		EMPIRE SPRAY
PRIMROSE HILL		EMPIRE STANLEY
		EASTERN CITY
		DAGHESTAN
		DALTON HALL
		HELENCREST
		KAFIRISTAN
		NOVELIST

(Note: MICHAEL E differed in that her aircraft was a Sea Hurricane of 804 Squadron, with a naval pilot)

882 Squadron on SEARCHER'S flight deck—hangar cleaning in progress   [*D. J. Frearson*

A fine study of a Firefly FR 1 of 746A Flight crossing SEARCHER'S round-down.   This ship was
the only CVE to embark the type for operations   [*D. J. Frearson*

Close co-operation between carrier aircraft and the surface escorts was the key to Atlantic anti-submarine operations. A rocket-armed Swordfish II of TRACKER's 816 Squadron orbits KITE as the sloop picks up survivors from one of the many U-boats sunk by Captain F. J. Walker's 2nd Escort Group   [IWM

ANCYLUS, a Merchant Aircraft Carrier, showing signs of wear forward. The single barrier is raised aft of the two Swordfish of 836 Squadron   [IWM

UNICORN accompanying MKF 15 from Gibraltar in June 1943, one of her few appearances in an operational role   [MoD (Admiralty)

Dawn readiness: one of 896 Squadron's Wildcat Vs picketed on PURSUER's catapult. The convoy is part of OS67/KMS 41 bound for Gibraltar from the UK in February 1944   [D. J. Frearson

8-K scrambled a few minutes after the above photograph was taken
                                                                    [D. J. Frearson

16th February 1944: Lieutenant (A) E. S. Erikson RNZNVR of 811 Squadron taxies up BITER's
deck after he and Lieutenant W. C. Dimes RNZNVR had shared a Ju 290A some 300 miles west
of Finisterre (Wildcat IV)   [IWM

The dusk patrol standing by on PURSUER (881 Squadron) before the launch which resulted
in the destruction of an He 177A and an Fw 200C on 12th February 1944   [IWM

TRACKER, with Avengers and Wildcats at readiness, accompanies BITER with OS68/KMS42 bound for Gibraltar in February 1944   [*MoD (Admiralty*)]

NAIRANA in "normal" North Atlantic operational conditions   [*IWM*

VINDEX passing through the spray of two depth charges jettisoned by one of her Swordfish; a Sea Hurricane IIC is parked forward. 825 Squadron sank two U-boats in the spring of 1944 while operating from VINDEX on hunter/killer sweeps   [IWM

A Swordfish of 825 Squadron on finals for VINDEX   [IWM

The Netherlands' MAC-ship MACOMA turning into wind within the convoy screen to recover an aircraft   *[Lt Cdr Van der Minne, R Neth. N*

Sub Lieutenant (A) R. Banks of 896 Squadron in close : 9th June 1944, on fighter patrol over the escort groups in the South Western Approaches   *[D. J. Frearson*

A Wildcat V of 896 Squadron is prepared for launching on
D-day, 6th June 1944. The SHAEF stripes were applied
overnight and on some aircraft the paint was so wet that
it ran or smeared on being catapulted

[*D. J. Frearson*

HS 187, a Blackburn-built Swordfish II of 860 Squadron aboard the Dutch MAC-ship GADILA. Although built as a Mark II, this aircraft has the later equipment fitted to Swordfish IIIs : centimetric ASV between the oleos as well as the older metric Yagi antennae on the outboard interplane struts. RATOG is fitted aft of the main under-carriage, necessary to get the aircraft airborne with its load of two 250lb AS depth charges and four marine markers off the short deck
[Lt Cdr Van der Minne

HS 187 lands back aboard GADILA. The width of the flight deck is not much greater than the aircraft's wing span
[Lt Cdr Van der Minne

Despite heavy movement on the ship and frequent snow-storms, FENCER's 842 Squadron sank three U-boats unassisted in a 48-hour period on 1st and 2nd May 1944. Two Wildcats and two R/P-armed Swordfish can be seen aft as the flight deck party clear the snow with brooms and shovels   [*IWM*

A Bv 138C is shot down by Lieutenant (A) J. G. Large RNVR against the background of the Arctic Ocean: 31st March 1944   [*IWM*

ACTIVITY in the Clyde between convoy operations: Swordfish and Wildcats of 819 Squadron
on deck   [*IWM*

U-288, her 37mm mounting out of action and only one barrel of the 20mm mounting firing, as
an Avenger of Tracker's 846 Squadron administers the coup de grace with depth charges, after
a Wildcat of the same squadron had strafed the gunners and a Swordfish of 819 had hit the
U-boat with rockets, preventing her from diving   [*IWM*

Below: An Avenger burns under TRACKER's after round-down after misjudging the approach. The fire was brought under control swiftly and the flying programme suffered no delay   [*IWM*

Right: EAGLE flies off her 813 and 824 Squadrons on an operational sortie
[*W. T. Speary*

Right: A Sea Gladiator of 813 Squadron's fighter flight takes off from EAGLE for a patrol over the Mediterranean Fleet. No dinghy is carried between the undercarriage legs, suggesting that this is either one of the 38 "interim" Sea Gladiators, or that the dinghy has been removed from a production aircraft to improve performance   [*J. W. G. Welham via R. C. Jones*

The pilot of one of EAGLE's Sea Gladiators (N5517) unstraps as the aircraft is manhandled aft to clear the hook from the arrester wire   [J. W. G. Welham via R. C. Jones

1st September 1940: ILLUSTRIOUS and VALIANT pass into the Eastern Mediterranean through the Sicilian Narrows. Seen from ARK ROYAL   [MoD (Admiralty)

ILLUSTRIOUS landing on her 815 and 819 Squadrons in the Eastern Mediterranean   [*IWM*

ILLUSTRIOUS listing and on fire—10th January 1941. One hole made by an 1,102lb armour
piercing bomb is to be seen to the starboard side of the centre line, while beyond the after lift
has been blown out of its well by the blast of bombs exploding in the hangar   [*IWM*

An Albacore releases its torpedo at FORMIDABLE during a practice strike.   Beneath the aircraft
can be seen the track of another "runner", probably dropped by the photographic aircraft
[/WM

Albacores of the naval pathfinding squadrons, 815 and 826, in flight over the Western Desert
in 1942.   None of the aircraft appears to be fitted with ASV radar, and the undersurfaces are doped
matt-black for night operations, as opposed to the standard Fleet Air Arm duck-egg blue.   (4A—
T9141, P—T9153, 4G—T9214)   *[/WM*

In February 1945 the enemy returned briefly to large-scale air torpedo attack, after a wholly unsuccessful small-scale attempt in December 1944. The employment of larger forces only led to larger losses suffered by the Luftwaffe; one straggler from RA 64 was sunk while the enemy lost a total of 21 aircraft, the Wildcats claiming four Ju 88s destroyed, with five others probably destroyed. The February attack was the last of any kind against Arctic convoys on the high seas, and the carrier aircraft could claim no further victories, although they covered three more round voyages.

Nowhere was the contribution of the escort carriers more noteworthy. The aircraft flew night and day, often in appalling weather. So well did they execute their duty that out of 749 merchant ships sailing in 27 carrier-escorted convoys only 24 were lost to enemy action. Of the 24, no fewer than 16 were sunk as far back as September 1942, out of the 55 ships in PQ 18/QP 14. To serve as a comparison, 63 ships were sunk by enemy action out of the 26 convoys sailing without carrier escort. The positive achievement included the sinking of 14 U-boats, nine of them by the unaided action of the aircraft, the other five in conjunction with the surface escorts.

The reason for the high proportion of aircraft kills was the poor performance of Asdic (Sonar) in the extremely cold waters, where layers of unequal temperature made detection of a submerged U-boat virtually impossible for the surface escorts. The aircraft therefore sought out the enemy at range and either destroyed him or left him crippled on the surface, to be finished off by gunfire. To illustrate the point, during the passage of RA 57 in March 1944 the escorting ships expended over 1,000 depth charges and "Hedgehog" projectiles to no avail (apart from the deterrent effect), while CHASER'S Swordfish fired less than 100 rocket projectiles to destroy two U-boats outright and so damage U-472 that it was unable to dive, being finished off by gunfire from ON-SLAUGHT.

The extreme air temperatures encountered deprived the carrier aircraft of further successes. Weapons' malfunctioning was fairly common: depth charge safety clips failed to release when frozen up, the acoustic A/S torpedo, known to the United States Navy as "Fido", often failed to run, and gun stoppages prevented the Sea Hurricanes and Wildcats from claiming more victories. As it was, they destroyed over 30 enemy aircraft in the course of their operations. About half of these were shadowers, the remainder being torpedo strike aircraft.

The cold also affected the Swordfish aircrew badly, flying as they were in aircraft with cockpits completely exposed to the elements. It was retained because of its ready availability, but principally because it was the only aircraft of its time which could operate with a modicum of safety from the small deck of an escort carrier in Arctic weather *by night*. Only TRACKER employed the Avenger in an opposed N. Russian convoy operation, and then the aircraft only flew by day. Consequently, the Swordfish accounted for all but one of each category of kill: eight outright, sharing the ninth; four out of the five "shared" kills.

The Fleet Air Arm lost nearly 80 aircraft of all types in Arctic convoy escort operations. The majority of the write-offs came in deck-landing accidents, inevitable in the prevailing conditions. Few aircrew lost their lives however; the planeguard destroyers rapidly became adept at rescuing aviators from the sea, seldom much above freezing.

Outline details of each operation are given in tabular form.

THE BATTLE OF THE ATLANTIC—THE ESCORT CARRIERS' CONTRIBUTION

With the fall of Continental Europe in the summer of 1940 the radius of action of not only the U-boats but also of the co-operating maritime patrol aircraft was extended by the acquisition of bases on the Atlantic coasts of both France and Norway. From the autumn of 1940 1/KG 40, operating Fw 200s from the excellent airfield at Bordeaux/Merignac, attacked convoys and individual ships out to 20° West; their main menace lay in their ability to detect, report, and shadow convoys far beyond the range of any aircraft of Coastal Command that could interfere with their activities. Once the convoys were detected, the aircraft homed U-boats to the scene, where the surface escorts were often too few to counter a "wolf-pack" attack.

The first stop-gap measure introduced by the Admiralty was the employment of the old catapult ship PEGASUS, together with several converted merchant ships, in the fighter catapult role. Fulmars and later Sea Hurricanes were embarked, between one and three aircraft to each ship, provided by 804 Squadron. Five Fighter Catapult Ships were commissioned into the Royal Navy, four of which saw service with convoys. A total of 10 launches was made in anger, with the destruction of one Fw 200C and the damaging of another in consequence. Four Fulmars managed to reach airfields ashore, the pilot of another was killed when he flew into a hillside in Ireland after a long flight back from the Atlantic. The remaining five pilots were rescued. The deterrent effect of the Fighter Catapult Ships was considerably as each launch resulted in the shadower's being driven off.

The operational life of the naval units was only 18 months, from December 1940 to June 1942, their place with the convoys being taken by the Catapult Armed Merchantmen. The latter differed in that they continued to fly the Red Ensign and with the exception of MICHAEL E they were provided with RAF aircraft and pilots. Between May 1941 and August 1943 the CAM ships sailed on 170 round voyages with Gibraltar, North Atlantic and Arctic convoys. Only eight operational launches were made, resulting in the destruction of six aircraft and the damaging of another three. EMPIRE MORN was the only CAM ship to launch twice, her successive aircraft destroying three of the enemy aircraft. Of the 35 Catapult Armed Merchant ships to enter service, 12 were lost while employed with the convoys.

Encouraged by the early successes of the Fighter Catapult ships, whose every launch resulted in the driving-off of shadowers, the Admiralty

DISPOSITION OF VESSELS AND SQUADRONS

The Battle of the Atlantic — Escort Carriers between September 1941 and 1944

Note: the Carriers are dealt with in the order in which they entered service

AUDACITY — September to December 1941: 2 round voyages to Gibraltar (lost on second return trip)

    802 Squadron   6 Martlet II (September and October)
    802   ,,   8 Martlet II (November and December)
Shared Kill: U-131 with STANLEY and others
Enemy aircraft destroyed: 5 Fw 200C. Carrier sunk 21/12/41

BITER — April 1943 to August 1944: 16 trans-Atlantic and Gibraltar convoys

    811 Squadron   9 Swordfish & 3 Wildcats (to October 1943)
    811   ,,   6 Swordfish & 6 Wildcats (to January 1944)
    811   ,,   11 Swordfish & 4 Wildcats (to August 1944)
Shared Kills: U-203 with PATHFINDER; U-89 with BROADWAY & LAGAN
Enemy aircraft destroyed: 1 Ju 290B in February 1944

ARCHER — May 1943 to July 1943: 3 trans-Atlantic convoys and 1 A/S sweep

    819 Squadron   9 Swordfish (8 in July)
    892 Squadron   3 Martlets (4 in July)
Kill: U-752

UNICORN — May and June 1943: 3 Gibraltar convoys

    818 Squadron   9 Swordfish
    824   ,,   9 Swordfish
    887   ,,   10 Seafires

TRACKER — September 1943 to June 1944: 12 trans-Atlantic and Gibraltar convoys and 2 A/S sweeps. Damaged in collision 6/44

    816 Squadron   9 Swordfish & 6 Seafires (to end of 1943)
    846   ,,   12 Avengers & 7 Wildcats (to June 1944)
(2 shared kills with Arctic convoys in April 1944)

FENCER — October 1943 to August 1944: 12 trans-Atlantic and Gibraltar convoys and 2 A/S sweeps

    842 Squadron   9 Swordfish and 6 Seafires (to November 1943)
    842   ,,   11 Swordfish & 4 Wildcats (9 fighters from February 1944)
Kill: U-666 (plus 3 sunk in Arctic). Enemy aircraft destroyed: 1 Fw 200C

STRIKER — December 1943 to July 1944: 9 Gibraltar convoys and 3 A/S sweeps

    824 Squadron   9 Swordfish & 6 Sea Hurricanes (to May 1944)
    824   ,,   12 Swordfish & 6 Wildcats

ACTIVITY — February to August 1944: 14 Gibraltar convoys and 1 A/S sweep

    819 Squadron   9 Swordfish & 3 Wildcats (February to April)
    833   ,,.   3 Swordfish & 7 Wildcats (to August)

NAIRANA–February 1944 to September 1944: 13 Gibraltar convoys and 1 A/S sweep

    835 Squadron   9 Swordfish and 6 Sea Hurricanes
Enemy aircraft destroyed: 2 Ju 290B in March 1944

PURSUER — (Fighter Carrier) — February and June 1944. 2 Gibraltar convoys and fighter cover for 2 A/S sweeps

    881 Squadron   10 Wildcats
    896   ,,   10 Wildcats
Enemy aircraft destroyed: 1 Fw 200C and 1 He 177A in February; 1 Ju 88 in June

VINDEX — March to August 1944: 2 Gibraltar convoys in March & 3 A/S sweeps

    825 Squadron   12 Swordfish & 6 Sea Hurricanes
Shared kills: U-653 with 2nd Escort Group; U-765 with 6th Escort Group
(plus one kill and 2 shared kills in the Arctic)

SEARCHER — (Fighter Carrier) June 1944: 2 Gibraltar convoys

    882 Squadron   10 Wildcats
    898   ,,   10 Wildcats

EMPEROR — (Assault Carrier) — June 1944: 1 Gibraltar convoy and 1 A/S sweep

    800 Squadron   10 Hellcats
    804   ,,   10 Hellcats

CAMPANIA — June to August 1944: 6 Gibraltar convoys

    813 Squadron   12 Swordfish & 4 Wildcats

DISPOSITION—continued

ASSAULT CVEs escorting convoys while en route for operations in the Mediterranean

BATTLER — June 1943: 2 Gibraltar convoys
    835 Squadron   9 Swordfish & 6 Sea Hurricanes
    808A Flight   4 Seafires
Enemy aircraft destroyed: 1 Fw 200C in June
HUNTER — August 1943: 1 Gibraltar convoy
    834 Squadron   6 Swordfish & 6 Seafires
STALKER — October 1943: 1 return convoy
    833 Squadron   6 Swordfish
ATTACKER — October 1943: 1 return convoy
    879 & 886 Squadrons — Seafires
(Note: ATTACKER probably had no more than half a dozen serviceable aircraft)
HUNTER, STALKER & ATTACKER repeated the U.K. to Gibraltar convoys in May 1944, prior to their employment in Operation "Dragoon" in August 1944. Aircraft complement at this period is in appropriate section.)

The Battle of the Atlantic — Merchant Aircraft Carriers
Note: The ships are listed in the order in which they entered service; figures in parenthesis indicates the number of attacks made by aircraft from the ship.

Grain Ships	Tankers
1943:	1943:
EMPIRE MACALPINE (2) May	RAPANA (1) July
EMPIRE MACANDREW (2) July	AMASTRA September
EMPIRE MACRAE September	ACAVUS October
EMPIRE MACCALLUM (1) December	ANCYLUS (1) October
EMPIRE MACKENDRICK (1) December	EMPIRE MACKAY October
	EMPIRE MACCOLL (1) November
	EMPIRE MACMAHON December
	EMPIRE MACCABE (1) December
	ALEXIA December
1944:	1944:
EMPIRE MACDERMOTT (1) March	MIRALDA (3) January
	ADULA February
	GADILA (R.Neth.N) (1) March
	MACOMA (R.Neth.N) May

Action was taken on 12 occasions by MAC Swordfish, there being 2 ships involved on 3 of these occasions.
MIRALDA was employed for training until the Spring of 1944.
The Swordfish of 836, 840 and 860 (Royal Netherlands Navy) Squadrons provided all detachments, the parent station being Maydown in Ulster.

---

resurrected a pre-war plan and requested the conversion of the first of the auxiliary aircraft carriers, later dubbed escort carriers. The ex-German prize HANNOVER was re-named AUDACITY and was given a 460ft flight deck, fitted with two arrester wires and a barrier, over the existing hull. She was flush-decked, with no provision for a hangar, so that all stowage and servicing was in the open air.

The sturdy Martlet II was selected as her main armament, up to eight being embarked, the first of the type to go to sea in squadron strength. 802 Squadron began operations from AUDACITY in September 1941 and although the ship made only two round voyages on the Gibraltar route, her aircraft revolutionised the concept of carrier trade protection. Three of the four convoys were opposed by the enemy, and the Martlets destroyed five Fw 200C shadowers, damaged three, and drove off a ninth in the course of the three operations. The fighters were also used for anti-submarine patrols, reporting nine U-boats in all; one of these, U-131, was shared with the destroyers of the surface escort, the aircraft being lost to the return fire from the U-boat. One other Martlet was lost to the fire of a Fw 200 dorsal gunner, and the ship herself was sunk in the middle of a fierce A/S battle on the night of 21st December 1941.

Despite AUDACITY's immediate success, the next British conversion did not enter service until February 1944; the Royal Navy relied upon the supply of American-built escort carriers (CVEs) while the British yards concentrated upon the construction of corvettes, frigates, etc. The first American-built escort carriers did not enter service with the Royal Navy until the late summer of 1942 and although AVENGER gave close cover to an Arctic convoy in September 1942, they did not begin trade protection operations in the Atlantic until late April 1943.

The delay was imposed by the need for carriers to support the North African invasion in November 1942, followed by refits and modifications found to be essential in the light of early experience. The need for frequent refit was a drawback experienced with this type of ship, the hull and propulsion of which were not designed for the treatment received as a warship. The modifications were mainly to the aviation gasoline system, to bring it up to the standards demanded by the Admiralty. The loss of AVENGER by fire and explosion after sustaining one torpedo hit, and the aviation gasoline explosion which destroyed DASHER in March 1943, stressed the need for improvement. With the addition of ballast and electronics, the programme took up to three months to effect after delivery to shipyards in the United Kingdom. Two CVEs were torpedoed after the modification programme was started and neither was sunk, despite severe damage; AMEER was damaged by Kamikaze in July 1945, the only Royal Navy CVE to suffer from this form of attack, but she was returned to service within weeks. Their American counterparts suffered heavily from all kinds of attack, and in some cases their loss might have been avoided if they had incorporated the Royal Navy's alterations.

BITER was the first of the escort carriers to commence regular trade protection operations in the North Atlantic, sailing for her first convoy support mission in April 1943, just a month after the USS BOGUE had begun A/S operations.

Yet again success came quickly, a Swordfish of 811 Squadron sharing U-203 with the destroyer PATHFINDER on 25th April. Although BITER covered another 16 convoys between then and August 1944, her only other positive success came hot on the heels of the first, when 811 shared U-89 with the 5th Escort Group. ARCHER joined the Battle of the Atlantic in May 1943 and on 23rd of the same month a Swordfish of her 819 Squadron became the first aircraft to sink a U-boat with rockets, U-752 being the victim. ARCHER was unfortunately plagued by machinery defects throughout her brief career and was reduced to Care and Maintenance in October 1943, after just one more Atlantic A/S operation.

Meanwhile the tempo of CVE operations had increased rapidly. By June 1943, four escort carriers were with convoys and this figure had grown to seven by the end of the year. Cover was extended to the Gibraltar routes, and the number of merchant ships sunk by U-boats fell off dramatically. The U-boats themselves were moved away from mid-Atlantic, where the "Gap" was at last closed, and into the South Atlantic, the Indian Ocean and the Arctic.

No further Fleet Air Arm successes against U-boats were registered after May 1943, until February 1944, when FENCER's 842 Squadron sank U-666 in the Eastern Atlantic. The US Navy's CVE groups were operating to the south of the Royal Navy's operational areas, and in these warmer, less disturbed waters, enjoying better conditions of visibility, cloud cover and sea state, their Avengers sank 28 U-boats in the eight months. The bulk of these successes were obtained off the Azores, an area favoured by the operational U-boats and their "milch-cows" for re-fuelling. American tactical doctrine differed radically from the British and Canadian thought in that from the outset their groups conducted "Hunter/Killer" sweeps across the main convoy routes rather than sustained convoy escort and support. The Royal Navies, on the other hand, favoured the latter, believing that close cover throughout the passage of convoys through known danger areas would result in increased safety for the merchant ships. Many U-boats were thus sighted and driven down, while the CVE was unable to prosecute the contact owing to the need to continue on with the convoy.

By March 1944, however, the Royal Navy had sufficient escort carriers available to enable ships to be spared for the first major anti-submarine sweep since September 1939. The newly-commissioned VINDEX, with the experienced 825 Squadron embarked, was chosen for the hunter/killer operation; working with the 6th Escort Group in the South West Approaches she met foul weather but flew her aircraft day and night. The Swordfish made several promising attacks and on 15th March 1944 her aircraft co-operated with Captain F. J. Walker's 2nd Escort Group, which had just joined the force, to destroy U-653 in a night attack. This success was followed on 6th May, while VINDEX was on her second sweep, U-765 being shared with the American-built escorts BLIGH, BICKERTON and AYLMER. Although the sweeps proved to be successful, the cost was prohibitive. Aircraft and aircrew losses were high, as was to be expected when flying was conducted by day and night from a small carrier in the North Atlantic. There were only just enough aircrews to man the 18 Swordfish and Sea Hurricanes, allowing little time for rest, and the flight deck handling crews were grossly under-manned. All personnel were exhausted at the end of the second operation, while the ship herself required a two-month re-fit.

The United States Navy suffered few of the disadvantages experienced by the Fleet Air Arm. As already related, the weather was more clement in their areas, the U-boats more numerous, and in the Avenger they had a better *day* search and strike aircraft, which was not only faster and more comfortable than the old Swordfish, but was also more rugged, an essential quality for the rough and tumble of winter escort carrier operations. Up to 50% spare aircrew were borne, and their flight deck crews averaged 80 trained men as against the 20-odd impressed seamen, stokers and Marines to be found doing the same job in their British sister-ships. The one field in which the Fleet Air Arm was pre-eminent was in night operation and in the use of radar for night and bad weather search, detection and attack.

Fighters were embarked in every trade protection escort carrier, and the Martlets, Sea Hurricanes and Seafires were used to the full. On the Gibraltar run they were often called upon to act in their intended role, as interceptors, but in the Atlantic they were generally used as part of a strike team in co-ordinated attacks on surfaced U-boats. One CVE, PURSUER, was indeed introduced on the Gibraltar route as purely a Fighter carrier. Her Wildcats distinguished themselves in February 1944 when they carried out a dusk attack on a mixed force of He 177 and Fw 200 glider-bomb parent aircraft. One aircraft of each type was destroyed and the remainder driven off, all the Wildcats returning safely to PURSUER. The fighters from A/S carriers also had their successes, BITER's and FENCER's Wildcats had a success apiece on the Gibraltar convoy route in early 1944, shooting down a Ju 290 and an He 177 respectively, while Sea Hurricanes from NAIRANA's 835 Squadron shot down a pair of Ju 290s. The operational life of the Seafire in the CVEs was limited, the weak undercarriage and narrow wheel track rendered the type unsuitable for extended operations in rough weather.

The use of the fighters in A/S strike teams was entirely successful. As soon as it was realized that U-boats were prepared, in some cases, to remain on the surface to fight it out with the aircraft, the tactics employed by the composite squadrons were adapted to deal with the new situation. As the Swordfish and, to a lesser extent, the Avenger, were vulnerable when committed to an attack, the fighters were maintained at a state of readiness on deck and flown off on receipt of a sighting report. As the strike aircraft made its run with rockets, bombs or depth charges, the fighter strafed the U-boats' flak mounts, keeping the gunners' heads down. Sea Hurricanes were even armed with rocket projectiles to combine both roles, disconcerting the flak while delivering a lethal attack. The fighters alone never achieved a kill, although Sea Hurricanes on the Arctic route did damage U-boats sufficiently to force them to return to base. The Wildcat was by far the best of the CVE-borne fighters, combining a respectable low-level performance with a sturdy airframe and undercarriage, which allowed it to operate, on occasion, in conditions unsuitable for even the Swordfish.

MERCHANT AIRCRAFT CARRIERS

The Merchant Aircraft Carriers were conceived at the time of AUDACITY's conversion. A simple flight-deck was constructed over the existing superstructure of a tanker or grain carrier and fitted with a safety barrier and two or three wires. The grain carriers were given a lift and a small hangar and could carry four Swordfish, whereas the tankers had no hangar but a rather longer flight deck, the aircraft complement being reduced to three aircraft in some cases. Both types of conversion continued to serve as merchant ships, with a naval cell on board, flying a merchant ensign and carrying in excess of 80% of their normal cargo capacity.

The first MAC ship sailed with a convoy in May 1943, just a month after the first CVE had entered service in the North Atlantic. Within a year there were 18 merchant aircraft carriers operational on the North Atlantic and Gibraltar convoy routes, two of them flying the Netherlands' merchant ensign. Only the Swordfish was embarked operationally in the MAC ships, the aircraft being provided by three pool squadrons: 836, 840 and 860 (Royal Netherlands Navy) which by the beginning of 1944 mustered between them 92 Swordfish, many with MERCHANT NAVY stencilled on the aft fuselage in place of the standard ROYAL NAVY.

Up to four MAC ships were included in certain convoys, although two was the most common number. From the end of 1944, with the reduced threat from U-boats in ocean waters, the Merchant Aircraft Carriers began to revert to trade. A diminishing number continued to serve until the end of the War in Europe, and it was in some ways appropriate that the last operational flight by a Swordfish was made from the EMPIRE MACKAY on 28th June 1945.

Twelve attacks were carried out by aircraft from these ships in the course of 4,000 sorties. While the MAC ships' Swordfish enjoyed no success from these attacks, the U-boats had no success against any convoy including an MAC ship in its formation.

During the spring of 1944, 11 non-operational voyages were made by Merchant Aircraft Carriers, ferrying over 200 aircraft to the United Kingdom from America, as part of the pre-invasion build-up. CVEs were also used in this role, ferrying USAAF aircraft to Britain, as well as the Avengers, Corsairs, Hellcats and Wildcats required by the Fleet Air Arm.

The escort carriers did not enter the Battle of the Atlantic until the struggle was reaching its climax, but there seems little reason to doubt that their activities in closing the "Gap" tipped the scales in favour of the Allies. The Royal Navy's CVEs contributed to the destruction of six U-boats in their areas of responsibility in the North Atlantic, and many more were attacked inconclusively. The US Navy sank 35 all told, in a rather longer period of operations.

The combined effect of the joint anti-submarine offensive was that by the September of 1944 it was unnecessary to provide CVE protection for the Atlantic convoys and the experienced carrier staffs and aircrew were redeployed to other theatres of war where their expertise was in demand.

Section 2

THE MEDITERRANEAN FLEET

September 1939 to May 1941

The War did not begin in earnest in the Mediterranean until 10th June 1940, when Italy commenced hostilities. During the preceding nine months the Mediterranean Fleet was numerically weak, due to the pressing commitments in other theatres of operations: when the existence of enemy surface raiders in ocean waters was confirmed, GLORIOUS, the only aircraft carrier operational with the Fleet, was detached to search and patrol off Socotra, at the Indian Ocean entrance to the Red Sea. GLORIOUS returned to the Mediterranean in January 1940, after three months on this duty, in need of a re-fit. Hardly had that been completed when she was rushed home to participate in the Norwegian campaign, only to be lost two months later.

From October 1939 the old carrier ARGUS had been based at Hyères, near Toulon, availing herself of the favourable Mediterranean weather for the deck-landing training of Swordfish pilots. The instructors were drawn from the survivors of COURAGEOUS' 811 and 822 Squadrons, and their experience paid dividends in a manner unforeseen at the time of the formation of ARGUS' 767 Squadron. Shortly after Italy had entered the War, 767 Squadron flew from Hyères to bomb Genoa, using French bombs; this was one of the first offensive moves against Italy, France being fully pre-occupied with the German onslaught in the north of the country. After the raid the Swordfish flew to Malta, via Tunisia, and were re-numbered 830 Squadron. Flying from Hal Far (the southernmost airfield in Malta) for the succeeding 33 months, 830 achieved outstanding success in the night interdiction and shipping strike roles.

Meanwhile EAGLE had left Singapore for the Mediterranean in May 1940, after a long and extensive re-fit. She was ready to sail with Admiral Cunningham's Mediterranean Fleet in early July, having embarked three Sea Gladiators, held in reserve at Alexandria for GLORIOUS' 802 Squadron, to supplement the 18 Swordfish of 813 and 824 Squadrons. The Fleet sailed on 8th July and encountered the Italian Fleet in an inconclusive action off Calabria on the following day. Two Swordfish strikes were launched in the course of the skirmish, but as EAGLE had to provide virtually all the required reconnaissance, shadowing, gunnery spotting, fighter defence and striking force with just 21 aircraft, the few aircraft available had little chance of success in torpedo strikes on undamaged warships. Throughout their entire time at sea the Mediterran-

73

ean Fleet was the target of heavy, accurate air attacks, but thanks to the determination of the few Sea Gladiators, flown by Swordfish pilots, little damage was caused to the Fleet by day air attack. During the six months embarked in EAGLE, the Sea Gladiators destroyed seven enemy aircraft and damaged another three suffering in return only slight damage to one aircraft.

On 10th July, the day after the Action off Calabria, Swordfish of 813 Squadron made a dusk torpedo attack on Augusta, in Sicily, hoping to find the Italian Fleet there. Of the few targets present, a destroyer and a tanker were torpedoed, the former being sunk. 824 Squadron had better fortune while operating from shore bases in Egypt, sinking two destroyers, three submarines and a depot ship for the expenditure of nine torpedoes. Two strikes, one on Tobruk and another on Bomba were involved, in July and late August.

While disembarked the squadrons were far from idle, flying local patrols and strikes on Italian-held harbours in Cyrenaica. The latter were so successful that the enemy withdrew all his larger units to Benghazi and later Tripoli, where they were less well positioned for attacks on Allied shipping.

Embarked, the Swordfish squadrons provided anti-submarine cover and reconnaissance sorties in support of convoys between Malta and Alexandria and Port Said, while the fighters continued to break up air attacks. In view of the small capacity for effective maritime co-operation possessed by the Middle East Air Force and the nature of the war in the Mediterranean, where the enemy possessed a strong surface fleet, it was realized that a second aircraft carrier was required to enable the Mediterranean Fleet to develop its full potential under Admiral Cunningham.

ILLUSTRIOUS was therefore allocated to the Med. Fleet and after a short work-up in the Bermuda area, she was passed into the Eastern Basin of the Mediterranean as part of an intricate reinforcement and replacement operation. ILLUSTRIOUS was the first of the new class of armoured Fleet carriers: with up to four inches of flight deck armour and an armoured hangar deck and walls she was proof against any but the heaviest bombs, while her vertical armour was of heavy cruiser standard. Fitted from the beginning with RDF (radar) she was armed with the 15 Fulmars of 806 Squadron, a unit which had seen extensive service over the Channel while equipped with Skuas and which was now taking the Fulmar to sea for the first time. Her TSR squadrons, 815 and 819, were veterans of the anti-invasion strikes against the Dutch ports, and many of the aircrew had served previously in GLORIOUS' Swordfish squadrons in the Mediterranean. Among the stores which ILLUSTRIOUS brought to the Mediterranean Fleet were long-range overload fuel tanks for the Swordfish, enabling strikes to be mounted at ranges of up to 200 miles from the carriers.

With two carriers available Admiral Cunningham lost no time in making their presence felt. The Swordfish and Fulmars ranged from Rhodes in the east to Sfax in the west, dive-bombing airfields, mining harbours and harassing Axis lines of communications. In the harbours along the North African coast and in the sea-lanes the four carrier-based Swordfish squadrons, backed up by 830 Squadron in Malta, wreaked havoc on Mussolini's shipping, at slight cost to themselves. Only in the first strike on Rhodes, early in September 1940, were the TSR aircraft intercepted, losing four Swordfish from EAGLE's squadrons to Fiat CR 42s.

The Fulmars, while slow by contemporary German and British standards, were more than a match for the Italian shadowers and striking forces. Over a dozen Cant (Rd'A) 501 and 506B patrol aircraft, as well as nine Savoia Marchetti 79 bombers, were destroyed by 806 Squadron for the loss of just *one* Fulmar in combat. So successful were the fighters that for five months no major unit of the Med. Fleet was damaged in a daylight air strike, local air superiority lying with the carrier aircraft.

The best known and remembered feat of arms by aircraft of the Mediterranean Fleet was without doubt the night strike on the Italian battlefleet at Taranto, on the night of 11th/12th November, 1940. Scheduled originally for Trafalgar Day (21st October) 1940, a fire in ILLUSTRIOUS' hangar delayed the operation, for which EAGLE was not available after she had suffered damage to her aviation fuel system from recurrent near-misses. Six of the latter ship's aircraft were transferred to ILLUSTRIOUS to strengthen the available force, planned to consist of 21 aircraft, flown off in two ranges, at hourly intervals.

DISPOSITION OF VESSELS AND SQUADRONS

The Mediterranean Fleet — September 1939 to January 1941

GLORIOUS — detached to Indian Ocean — November 1939 to January 1940. Returned to the United Kingdom May 1940: no operations in Mediterranean

802 Squadron	12 Sea Gladiators	
812 ,,	12 Swordfish	
823 ,,	12 Swordfish	
825 ,,	12 Swordfish	

EAGLE — from East Indies — June 1940

813 Squadron	9 Swordfish and 3 Sea Gladiators
824 ,,	9 Swordfish

ILLUSTRIOUS — from 1st September 1940

806 Squadron	15 Fulmars
815 ,,	9 Swordfish
819 ,,	9 Swordfish
813 ,,	4 Swordfish—detached for Taranto strike
824 ,,	2 Swordfish—detached for Taranto strike

The Mediterranean Fleet — March to May 1941

FORMIDABLE

803 Squadron	12 Fulmars
806 ,,	Never more than 6 Fulmars
826 ,,	12 Albacores
829 ,,	9 Albacores

Both strikes were fully co-ordinated, flares being dropped to illuminate the anchorage for the torpedo-bombers, while dive-bombers created a diversion by bombing subsidiary targets. Unlike nearly every other successful strike undertaken by the Fleet Air Arm the raid on Taranto enjoyed no surprise, the enemy having been on the *qui vive* for some hours prior to the strike. Although met by heavy flak and a balloon barrage, the six torpedo bombers from the first strike of 12 aircraft obtained two hits on LITTORIO, damaging her severely, and a fatal hit on CONTE DI CAVOUR, which sank in shallow water. A third hit was probably obtained on LITTORIO but the torpedo failed to detonate. An hour later the second strike, of five torpedo-bombers and three bombers/flare-droppers, hit LITTORIO yet again and inflicted serious damage on CAIO DUILIO. The bombing aircraft of the two strikes wrecked the seaplane base, which provided many of the shadowing aircraft which had been such a nuisance to the Mediterranean Fleet, set fire to oil storage tanks, and obtained hits on warships, although two 250lb Semi-Armour-Piercing bombs which hit a destroyer and the cruiser TRENTO failed to explode. One Swordfish from each strike was lost, one of the crews being lost.

CAVOUR sank, and although she was raised during the following year she was not returned to service; LITTORIO was badly damaged and did not return to full service for more than six months; CAIO DUILIO had to be beached in a sinking condition, her repairs taking nearly eight months to effect. In less than one hour 11 torpedo-armed Swordfish had put out of action half of Italy's battlefleet, achieving for the loss of two lives more than had been achieved by the Grand Fleet at Jutland for the loss of over 6,000 Royal Navy personnel. The effect on the Italians was immediate: although they did not retire completely from the combatant scene, as the High Seas Fleet had done after Jutland, they withdrew the main body of their fleet to northern bases and it was used only circumspectly whenever the carriers were known to be at sea. In the Battle of Cape Spartivento, 16 days after Taranto, the Italian fleet fled from a favourable tactical position when ARK ROYAL's aircraft appeared.

Two further carrier operations were carried out before the end of 1940; ILLUSTRIOUS' Swordfish attacked airfields in the Aegean and the Dodecanese while EAGLE struck at the harbour of Tripoli, and then in December ILLUSTRIOUS' squadrons bombed Rhodes again before switching to a strike on a convoy off Sfax, 1,000 miles to the west, only three days later. In a night attack by six aircraft, two large Italian merchant ships bound for Cyrenaica with vital military stores were sunk by torpedo, at no cost to the Swordfish.

In addition to the attacks on the harbours, the Swordfish squadrons from both carriers were employed in the night interdiction and support roles in the Western Desert, tasks in which other Fleet Air Arm units specialised in later months. Effective from both shore bases and the carriers, the naval aircraft, and the Mediterranean Fleet generally, had by the end of 1940 gained such an ascendancy over the Italian Fleet and the Regia Aero-nautica that the shortage of naval aircraft was the only serious restriction on naval movements in the eastern Mediterranean. Always short of spares, aircraft deliveries lagged behind demand, although at this stage the bottleneck following upon the virtual suspension of construction of naval aircraft had not become apparent; the situation did not become really critical until the following spring.

Meanwhile the Germans had become increasingly dissatisfied with the setbacks experienced by the Italians in Cyrenaica, and with the apparent lack of direction in their partner's war-effort. Advance elements of the Afrika Korps arrived in Tripolitania before the end of 1940 and with them came the first units of the Luftwaffe. One such was Fliegerkorps X, armed with Ju 87 and 88 aircraft, which had just finished intensive training in the anti-shipping role, with particular emphasis on the tactics for dealing with carriers. In spite of their overall success in the Norwegian campaign, the German High Command was fully aware that the majority of the Allied air opposition had come from the carriers of the Home Fleet: in the Mediterranean there was, at the end of 1940, a balanced Fleet, built around two aircraft carriers, which was threatening to cut off the Italian armies in Africa from metropolitan Italy.

On 10th January 1941, while ILLUSTRIOUS was covering a convoy entering Valletta's Grand Harbour, the Sicilian-based Fliegerkorps X carried out a devastating attack, co-ordinated with an ineffectual Italian torpedo strike. The latter did however have the effect of drawing the patrolling Fulmars down to low level as the Ju 87s came to their "push-over" point 11,000 feet above and there was thus little that the fighters could do to prevent the first wave of dive-bombers from bombing the carrier, defended only by the Fleet's AA fire. She was hit by a total of six 500 kilogramme armour-piercing bombs and suffered underwater damage from three near-misses. ILLUSTRIOUS was put out of action with her steering gear crippled, her lifts badly damaged, and with severe fires burning, but there is no doubt that the armoured deck saved her from destruction: no other carrier took anything like the punishment and survived. After a short time completely out of control she headed for Malta, protected by VALIANT, WARSPITE, and her own Fulmars, which had refuelled at Malta. A later strike by Ju 87s inflicted no further damage, and they lost four of their number to the Fulmars.

ILLUSTRIOUS was again bombed while carrying out emergency repairs at Malta, receiving two more direct hits on 16th January and suffering serious damage to the bottom plating from the mining effect of near-misses on 19th. The Fulmars joined the few RAF Hurricanes on the island in the defence of their ship, and she eventually broke out on the evening of 23rd January, bound for the Suez Canal and virtual re-building above the main deck in Norfolk Navy Yard, in the United States. It was not until the end of 1941 that ILLUSTRIOUS returned to the United Kingdom.

The Mediterranean Fleet was now without an armoured carrier and faced with a formidable opposition. With the Luftwaffe in firm control of the Sicilian Narrows and with the Axis advancing east through Cyrenaica once more, many of the areas off the North African coast where the Fleet had operated with impunity were now unsafe by day. EAGLE was by now in need of a refit and was too small to supply the needs of the Fleet against a modern opponent. She was unarmoured, slow, and her inability to carry fighters without displacing the essential search and strike aircraft precluded her further use in the Central Basin. In February 1941 she sailed for her last operation in the Eastern Mediterranean, escorting a convoy between Port Said and the Piraeus. EAGLE's departure was delayed by the length of time taken to transfer her relief, FORMIDABLE, from the South Atlantic, and the older ship finally passed through the Suez Canal on April 13th.

FORMIDABLE was the only suitable replacement for ILLUSTRIOUS. She was the second of the armoured Fleet carriers and had only been in commission for three months in January 1941; up to the time of her redeployment she had been hunting for surface raiders off St. Helena. Her air group consisted of the 12 Fulmars of 803 Squadron, flown by experienced aircrew who had just converted to the type after a commission aboard ARK ROYAL with Skuas, and the 21 Albacores of 826 and 829 Squadrons, both of which had seen extensive action in the English Channel, both before and after Dunkirk, and were now taking this particular type of aircraft to sea for the first time.

While on passage up the east coast of Africa, opportunity was taken to strike at the port of Mogadishu, Italian Somaliland, in support of the Commonwealth campaign in East Africa. As enemy air-laid mines were making the Suez Canal impassable in mid-February, the squadrons followed up the Mogadishu strike, which had taken place on 2nd, with attacks on the Italian naval base at Massawa in Eritrea. Bomb, torpedo and mining attacks were made on port installations on 13th and 21st February and 1st March 1941, but only minor damage was inflicted, as the enemy had not yet concentrated all his remaining force in Massawa. Early in April EAGLE's squadrons, awaiting the passage of their ship through the Canal, were flown to Port Sudan to support the final advance to the Red Sea by the Commonwealth troops. In the space of a fortnight the dozen or so aircraft sank three destroyers and drove two more ashore to be finished off by the guns of KINGSTON. Severe damage was inflicted upon the port installations and the local defences by the Swordfish, materially assisting the advancing forces. At the end of the campaign the squadrons, 824 and 813, rejoined EAGLE at Suez and proceeded into the Atlantic for trade protection duties; their contribution to Allied successes in the war against Italy had been out of all proportion to their numbers.

FORMIDABLE had meanwhile passed through the Suez Canal on 10th March and after a brief stay at Alexandria she sailed with the Fleet to cover a Malta convoy. On 17th March her Albacores attacked shipping in Tripoli, sinking a freighter, while 803s Fulmars shot down a couple of shadowers. FORMID's own fighter squadron had been reinforced by the remnants of 806 Squadron, the half-dozen Fulmars remaining after the damaging of ILLUSTRIOUS and the defence of Malta in January.

Armed with an armoured carrier once more, the Mediterranean Fleet lost no time in seeking out the Italian Fleet. Late on 27th March a Malta-based Sunderland sighted the enemy heading towards Crete, and Admiral Cunningham took his Fleet out from Alexandria in pursuit. At dawn on the following day the carrier's Albacores sighted and began to shadow the enemy ships, which had sortied with the intention of disrupting British convoys between Egypt and Greece, where the Italians were finding the campaign more arduous than anticipated. The shadowing continued all day, in the course of which the enemy were subjected to repeated air attacks, both from FORMIDABLE's torpedo aircraft and from the Swordfish of 815 Squadron, based at Maleme in Crete; medium-level bombing attacks by RAF aircraft did no damage but served the useful purpose of distracting the flak from the torpedo bombers. In the second strike an Albacore managed to put a torpedo into VITTORIO VENETO, reducing the battleship's speed to about eight knots; four hours later she had made the essential repairs and was capable of 19 knots, making good her escape, albeit by a narrow margin.

The last strike of the day, executed as darkness fell, was on a heavy cruiser division and one hit on POLA brought her to a standstill. Admiral Iachino, the Italian C-in-C, was unaware that Admiral Cunningham was still hot on his heels, the Fulmars having efficiently denied enemy reconnaissance aircraft all knowledge of the Royal Navy's whereabouts throughout the day, and he accordingly ordered POLA's sistership, ZARA and FIUME, together with two destroyers, to remain behind and stand by her until she could get underway once more. In the early hours of 29th March 1941 all five Italian ships were surprised and overwhelmed by the 15in guns of WARSPITE, VALIANT and BARHAM. The cost to the Royal Navy was just one Albacore and its crew.

In the Battle of Matapan the aircraft carrier had at last fulfilled the naval planners' intentions—torpedo aircraft had slowed elements of an enemy fleet by air strike, enabling the big guns of the Fleet to deliver the *coup de grace*. Only once again was this realized on the grand scale, with the destruction of BISMARCK after her damaging by ARK ROYAL's Swordfish in mid-Atlantic, two months after Matapan.

Three weeks after the battle the Albacores were in action again from the ship. They provided bombardment spotting for a shoot by the battleships against targets in the harbour of Tripoli and in the town itself. The dawn attack resulted in the destruction of five or six enemy ships and in considerable damage to local installations and dumps. Early in May FORMIDABLE escorted a particularly hard-fought Malta convoy, her Fulmars claiming seven enemy aircraft shot down. These operations resulted in particularly serious attrition in her fighter complement, already below strength, and on return to Alexandria on 12th May 1941 only four Fulmars were serviceable. Due to the inadequate supply position, caused partly by the production bottleneck referred to previously, FORMIDABLE was unable to make up her official complement until 25th May, when she sailed to take part in the battle for Crete with 12 patched-up aircraft embarked. The shortage did not only affect the Fulmar squadrons; as early as the Battle of Matapan, Swordfish had to be embarked to make up the numbers of TSR aircraft on board, the Albacores being in short supply in the Middle East.

While FORMIDABLE had been engaged in these operations, other Fleet Air Arm squadrons had seen hard fighting in the campaign for Greece. After the damaging of ILLUSTRIOUS in January 1941, her Swordfish were amalgamated to form one squadron, 815, which supported 830 Squadron's night anti-shipping offensive from Malta through January and February, before withdrawing to Maleme to rest and re-equip. With the German intervention in the Balkans seven Swordfish were detached to Eleusis in Greece, with the object of striking at enemy lines of communication between Brindisi and Valona. Between 13th March and 23rd April the Fleet Air Arm aircraft torpedoed 10 Axis merchant ships, five of which sank with their urgently needed supplies. In addition, the flight that had been left behind at Maleme for local patrols took part in the Battle of Matapan, although one pilot, Lieutenant F. M. A. Torrens-Spence, flew from Eleusis to lead one of the Maleme strikes on VITTORIO VENETO. With the evacuation of Allied forces from Greece, 815 Squadron fell back on Crete, later going on to Egypt.

805 Squadron was formed in Egypt in January 1941 for defence of coastal convoys and the Fleet base at Alexandria. In March it was moved to Maleme where the primitive operating conditions and the requirement for daily patrols over the mass of shipping between Greece and Egypt whittled down its strength until, on 15th May, only three Fulmars and three Gladiators out of the dozen or so which had arrived were serviceable. A flight of three Hurricanes was taken over when the RAF were evacuated on the same day, but by 17th May only the Hurricanes remained, the sole fighter defence for Crete. These three fighters intercepted a raid by 30 enemy aircraft on 17th, in the course of which six of the Axis bombers were claimed as destroyed, for the loss of all three Hurricanes. The two surviving pilots were evacuated on 19th May, so that when the airborne invasion commenced on the following day, the defenders were totally without air cover.

FORMIDABLE sailed on 25th May with the 12 Fulmars which she had been able to scrape together and a reduced complement of Albacores. To provide assistance by attacking the enemy airfield from which most of the raids on the defences of Crete were coming, the carrier launched a dawn strike against Scarpanto at dawn on 26th May. The attack achieved complete surprise and enemy aircraft on the ground were destroyed, but the small scale of the strike, limited by the availability of aircraft, robbed it of the full possible effects.

On retirement after recovering the strike, FORMIDABLE was attacked in the afternoon by a force of 30 Ju 87s of II/KG 30, operating not from Scarpanto, which was outside the effective range of Middle East Air Force, but from airfields in North Africa. Although the small Fulmar patrol managed to destroy four of the Stukas, the carrier was hit fore and aft by two 500kg armour-piercing bombs and received severe underwater damage aft from a near-miss. The damage overall was serious and well beyond the limited facilities available at Alexandria, so that after emergency repairs had been effected FORMIDABLE left the Mediterranean via the Suez Canal, to join ILLUSTRIOUS in the Norfolk Navy Yard.

After FORMIDABLE's passage through the Canal, on 24th July 1941, no other carrier saw action in the Eastern Mediterranean for 38 months, and no other Fleet carrier served there, except for brief work-ups prior to deployment with the Eastern Fleet. Air cover for the Mediterranean Fleet was henceforward provided by No. 201 Naval Co-operation Group of the Middle East Air Force, of which the disembarked naval squadrons were a part. Such cover was inadequate, partly because the RAF AoC continued to exercise operational control over the Group, with the result that the naval squadrons were seldom used to their full advantage, contributing more to MEAFs offensives than to the defence of the weakened Fleet.

Three strike squadrons and two fighter squadrons took part in the Syrian campaign, flying from bases in Palestine and Cyprus. They saw a considerable amount of action in June and July 1941: 803, 806 and 829 Squadrons flew from Ramat David in support of the Allied drive into Syria, while 815 and 826 added to their laurels by sinking and damaging by torpedo several Vichy and Axis ships, the squadrons being based at Nicosia.

With the successful conclusion of the campaign the squadrons were withdrawn to Egypt to rest and re-equip. The exception was 829 Squadron which re-armed with six Swordfish and sailed with FORMIDABLE to afford the carrier A/S protection during her long passage to the USA. The two Fulmar squadrons were equipped with ex-RAF Hurricanes and joined 805, re-armed with Martlet IIIs after the fall of Crete, to form the Naval Fighter Wing. Controlled by the Air Force. this Wing was used extensively over the land front where it enjoyed a fair amount of success, constituting as it did about 15% of the available Allied fighter strength.

The TSR squadrons were employed initially on coastal patrols but later, as their specialised merits were recognized, the Albacores were detailed for "pathfinding" duties, to illuminate targets behind the enemy front lines for bombing by MEAF Wellingtons and by themselves. The naval Observers' training, orientated towards long flights over the sea, was well suited to navigation over the Desert and they succeeded in a manner which the RAF Navigators could not emulate. 815, 821 and 826 Squadrons made up more than 40% of the Commonwealth night bombing strength and they denied the enemy any respite during the hours of darkness until after the Battle of Alamein, concentrating on the location, illumination and destruction of Axis' tank and motor transport laagers, and of motor transport bringing up supplies to the front-lines.

Section 3

FORCE H

June 1940 to November 1941

Force H was constituted on 28th June 1940, its functions being to cover those ocean areas left unguarded by the immobilisation of the French Fleet and to counter any westward movement by the Italian Fleet, particularly into the Atlantic. ARK ROYAL arrived five days before the formation of Force H, straight from the exhausting Norwegian campaign, to join HOOD as the nucleus of Admiral Somerville's force. RENOWN later replaced HOOD, and was joined by RESOLUTION but the strength of Force H was never as great as that possessed by the Mediterranean Fleet.

The first operation undertaken was the unhappy task of attempting to put the powerful French units at Oran out of action by force of arms, diplomacy having failed. On 3rd July ARK ROYAL's Swordfish spotted for a dawn bombardment by the capital ships and laid mines at the entrance to Mers-el-Kebir, the latter in an attempt to bottle up any French ships able to escape. The old battleship BRETAGNE blew up under the bombardment and DUNKERQUE was damaged and beached. The modern fast battleship STRASBOURG managed to slip past the mines and despite two strikes by the carrier aircraft she escaped to Bizerta. The first strike, by six bomb-armed Swordfish, was met with heavy anti-aircraft fire and two were lost for no success; a torpedo strike by six more Swordfish achieved surprise and lost none of the aircraft attacking but due to the small number of aircraft engaged and the poor tactics adopted they did not obtain any hits. The lack of current practice in torpedo attack continued to plague ARK ROYAL's TSR squadrons and the Fleet Air Arm as a whole, for many months to come.

As there was no obvious damage to DUNKERQUE, hard aground in Oran harbour, Admiral Somerville decided to disable her by means of carrier aircraft torpedo strike. On 6th July six Swordfish of 820 Squadron attacked the battleship and although the only torpedo to hit DUNKERQUE failed to explode, a hit was obtained on an ammunition lighter alongside and the resulting explosion caused severe damage to the battleship. Two follow-up strikes by Swordfish escorted by Skuas scored one more hit on the ship. These later strikes were opposed by Vichy Morane-Saulnier 406 and Curtiss Hawk 75 fighters which completely out-performed the Skuas, but which did not press their attacks; only one Skua was lost and the crew was rescued.

While Force H was attacking Oran, HERMES was shadowing the recently-commissioned battleship RICHELIEU. The shadowing had been going on for a fortnight and there was at one time a short-lived scheme for capturing her on the high seas. After RICHELIEU had taken refuge at Dakar in French West Africa, it was decided to put her out of action by means of a torpedo strike. This was executed shortly after dawn on 8th July 1940 by six Swordfish of HERMES' 814 Squadron. The attack was delivered between two rows of merchant ships, across a strong tide, in the face of AA fire, and obtained a single hit aft on the battleship. This one hit inflicted considerable damage on RICHELIEU: the propeller shafts were twisted, the steering gear damaged, and extensive flooding was caused aft. With the limited repair facilities at Dakar she was out of action for over a year, although her main armament was still intact and she could have got under way in an emergency.

Unaware that RICHELIEU's damage was serious, plans were drawn up for a further series of strikes, coupled with a Free French amphibious landing to the south of Dakar. Operation "Menace" began on September 23rd with the despatch of Free French envoys to the local airfield in ARK'S Swordfish and in two Caudron Luciolles embarked for the purpose. The mission was unsuccessful and offensive operations were accordingly commenced. The landings had been planned on the premise that the Vichy French would not oppose their fellow-countrymen, and might even defect from the Vichy cause; the premise was false and the amphibious operation proved to be a fiasco.

ARK ROYAL's air strikes were hampered by poor visibility and by the strong reaction by the defences. In particular, air opposition mounted and by the second day the Swordfish were unable to operate in the face of the fighters, while the Skuas were hard put to defend themselves without the added burden of looking after the slow TSRs. Little damage was inflicted either on RICHELIEU or on the three light cruisers which had joined her since the July strike, although several torpedo and dive-bombing attacks were mounted. The result of the expenditure of a considerable amount of 15in ammunition by the capital ships of Force H was one "possible" hit on RICHELIEU and another on a shore battery. The French battleship's gunnery had meanwhile been excellent: BARHAM was hit by several heavy shells and near-miss damage was inflicted on other ships. On 25th RESOLUTION was torpedoed and had to withdraw: this attack, coupled with increasingly accurate bombing by Martin 167s and the lack of success enjoyed by ARK ROYAL's aircraft, persuaded the Force Commander, Vice Admiral J. H. D. Cunningham, that little was to be gained from the continuation of the operation. Accordingly, "Menace" was abandoned in the early afternoon of 26th September 1940.

Dakar had seen the first use of the carrier in the amphibious support role, where all air cover had to be provided from the ship. The presence of only one carrier inevitably slowed flying operations but HERMES, which had also been intended for the operation, was damaged in collision with the AMC CORFU in August 1940, and was under repair at the time of "Menace". The aircraft themselves were not up to the task of providing the needed support, and never again were Swordfish used again as the principal strike aircraft against defended targets in full daylight. The Skuas were no match for the faster Vichy fighters and although they managed occasionally to break up bombing raids, they failed to destroy any of their opponents; with the Swordfish incapable of undertaking the needed reconnaissance missions, the Skuas were given this added task, insufficient aircraft thus remaining for fighter patrols and strike sorties.

Mediterranean Operations

Between the Oran and Dakar operations Force H made one sortie into the western Mediterranean to cover the first aircraft ferry operation by ARGUS. In common with all the later reinforcement operations, the RAF aircraft were flown off from a position to the west of Sicily, well within range of Malta. While ARGUS was flying off the 12 Hurricanes, accompanied by two Skuas for navigational assistance, ARK ROYAL's Swordfish attacked Cagliari airfield (Sardinia), on 2nd August, where they destroyed four hangars and four aircraft on the ground; three other Swordfish mined Cagliari harbour. There was no reaction on the part of the Italian fleet, but the Skuas were called upon to drive off shadowers, scoring their first victories against the Regia Aeronautica in the process.

The remainder of August was spent in the Atlantic, guarding against a possible break-out by RICHELIEU from Dakar, not appreciating that HERMES' strike of 8th July had rendered her unfit for sea. On 1st September ARK's Swordfish again bombed a Sardinian airfield, Elmas, as a diversionary measure for the passage of ILLUSTRIOUS through the Narrows to the Mediterranean Fleet.

After the Dakar debacle, in which she had lost nine aircraft through enemy action, ARK ROYAL returned to the United Kingdom for a short re-fit. When she returned to Gibraltar at the beginning of November her fighter strength was considerably augmented by the replacement of 803 Squadron's Skuas by the Fulmars of 808. On 9th November 1940 her aircraft delivered yet another diversionary attack on Sardinian airfields, as part of the build-up to a series of operations which culminated with the strike on Taranto by aircraft from ILLUSTRIOUS two days later.

On 17th November another strike, on Alghero airfield, whence the Italians had moved units after the earlier attacks on other bases in Sardinia, had to be called off due to bad weather in the western Mediterranean. The operation was intended to cover another ferry trip by ARGUS; 12 Hurricanes and two Skuas were flown off to the west of the Sicilian Narrows, but owing to fuel management problems only one Skua and four Hurricanes reached Malta.

Fortunately this proved to be the last ferry operation required for Malta through the Mediterranean for several months. The Takoradi route—the Gold Coast, Lagos, Fort Lamy (French Equatorial Africa), and Khartoum to Egypt— was now a practical proposition, and so ARGUS and FURIOUS were employed over the winter months in ferrying Hurricanes from Britain to West Africa. Commonwealth advances in the Western Desert through Cyrenaica put advanced fighter

DISPOSITION OF VESSELS AND SQUADRONS

Force H — Western Mediterranean operations August 1940 to April 1941
ARK ROYAL

800 Squadron	12 Skuas	
808 „	12 Fulmars (replaced 803 Squadron — October 1940)	
810 „	12 Swordfish	
818 „	9 Swordfish	
820 „	9 Swordfish	

ARGUS — ferry operations
821X Flight   3 Swordfish (for A/S protection)

Force H — Western Mediterranean Operations — April 1941 to November 1941

ARK ROYAL — torpedoed by U-81, 13th November 1941 and sank on 14th

807 Squadron	12 Fulmars	
808 „	12 Fulmars	
825 „	9 Swordfish (replaced 820 Squadron in June 1941)	
816 „	9 Swordfish (replaced 818 Squadron in July 1941)	
812 „	12 Swordfish (replaced 810 Squadron in September 1941)	

Note: Squadrons participating in the BISMARCK hunt were—807, 808, 810, 818, 820

ARGUS — ferry operations until November 1941

812 Squadron	12 Swordfish (April and May 1941)	
800Y Flight	3 Fulmars (May and June 1941)	
812 Squadron	4 Swordfish (November)	
807 „	4 Fulmars (November)	

FURIOUS — ferry operation June 1941
816 Squadron   9 Swordfish
VICTORIOUS — ferry operation June 1941
Aircraft complement as in BISMARCK hunt

---

airfields within range of Malta and the Hurricanes were flown through fully modified for "hot" operations.

On 27th November 1940 Force H had an unsatisfactory brush with the Italian fleet to the south-west of Sardinia. The Italians, with two of the battleships which had escaped damage at Taranto on 11th of the month, had the edge in capital ship and cruiser strength, and were in a favourable tactical position with Somerville's capital ships 100 miles apart and his cruisers dispersed. To add to the Royal Navy's embarrassment, there was a Malta convoy to be protected and the scene of the action was within easy reach of the enemy bombers based in Sardinia. ARK ROYAL was the principal deterrent—the activities of the two carriers in the Eastern Basin having made a vigorous impression on the Italian Navy. Three strikes were launched by ARK in an attempt to equalise the odds, and with the appearance of the carrier aircraft the enemy reversed his course and made for Cagliari. The first strike, by 11 torpedo aircraft, believed that they had obtained a hit on a LITTORIO class battleship, but owing to communications shortcomings Admiral Somerville did not learn of this until the action had been broken off an hour later. Meanwhile the Italians, who were making off at high speed, were harassed by another strike of nine Swordfish, which made a torpedo strike against a cruiser division. This was followed by a Skua strike against the same objective which obtained two near-misses and inflicted the only damage caused by the entire series of air strikes.

In this action the effect of ARK's Swordfish strikes had been diminished by the lack of specialized strike training. The Italians on their side had shown their respect for the Fleet Air Arm aircraft by their hasty retreat, and the effect of the encounter was to lead to even less activity on the part of the Italian Fleet.

The Fulmars and Skuas of the fighter patrols did well, breaking up several enemy air attacks and destroying a number of enemy aircraft. A lone Skua bounced and drove off five S.M. 79s ,their bombs jettisoned, even though the bombers completely out-performed the fighter. The direction of fighters by radar, pioneered during the Norwegian campaign, was now the vital factor in the defence of the Fleet and the fighters were scoring freely, within the limits of their performance.

One more convoy was escorted to Malta in 1940. The Italians made no attempt to interfere, so great was the moral ascendancy of the Royal Navy at the end of the year; the usual air attacks on Force H were beaten off by the Fleet fighters, and although ARK ROYAL herself was the primary target of many of the raids, she came through undamaged.

After the bombing of ILLUSTRIOUS on January 10th 1941, it was apparent that subsequent carrier operations within range of the Luftwaffe bases in western Sicily would be hazardous. As ARK ROYAL's protection and internal sub-division were not as complete as that in the more modern carriers she was employed in a rather more circumspect fashion from mid-January 1941. Early in the following month, however, ARK sailed with Force H to carry out a daring bombardment of Genoa. Before this operation the Swordfish carried out a torpedo strike on the Tirso Dam, in northern Sicily, but the strike, on 2nd February, failed due to a combination of bad weather, lack of local knowledge, and the strength of the dam. On 8th February RENOWN and MALAYA bombarded Genoa, spotting being provided by ARK's Swordfish; other Swordfish bombed factories in Genoa, mined the entrance to the Italian naval dockyard at La Spezia, and bombed targets in Pisa. The bombardment and air attacks were successful, both in the amount of damage inflicted and from the morale aspect. Force H enjoyed complete surprise and withdrew undetected, lending the raid more significance from the Italian viewpoint.

Preoccupation with the possibility of a break-out by the German naval squadron in Brest and the continued high level of Luftwaffe strength around the Sicilian Narrows led to ARK ROYAL's continuous employment to the west of the Straits of Gibraltar, and it was not until early April that she undertook her next Mediterranean operation, the ferrying of RAF Hurricanes to Malta. Two such missions were carried out in that month, another in May, and no less than three in June. Returning from the May operation, ARK was ordered into the Atlantic to cover a troop convoy from possible interference from the BISMARCK, which had broken out on the day of Force H's return to Gibraltar. As she was proceeding into mid-Atlantic with RENOWN, the carrier had another of her strokes of good fortune, passing close to U-556 which

had expended all its torpedoes. The subsequent crippling of the
BISMARCK by ARK's second strike is an everlasting tribute to the
flexibility of sea/air power; only six days had elapsed between the provision of much-needed fighters for Malta and the destruction of one of
the world's most powerful battleships more than 2,000 miles away. It
was particularly fitting that ARK ROYAL'S squadrons should vindicate
themselves after the disappointing results at the Battle of Cape Spartivento,
six months previously.

Force H participated in five convoy operations and eleven aircraft
ferry sorties between April and November 1941, ARK ROYAL being
supplemented variously by ARGUS, FURIOUS, and VICTORIOUS
in the transport of Hurricanes and, latterly, Blenheims. On one of
these operations the aircraft for Malta were in fact Albacores of 828
Squadron, which went on to operate from the island against Axis shipping
and targets in Sicily, Calabria and Tripolitania. In April 1941 the
nine Fulmars of 800X Squadron were flown off to Malta, where they
were used in the night-intruder role to the end of the year.

The replacement of the last Skua squadron by the Fulmars of 807
in April 1941 had given ARK an adequate fighter complement at
last, and the squadrons enjoyed considerable success against enemy
shadowers and bombers. Although the target of many bombing and
torpedo strikes ARK ROYAL was never damaged by enemy air attack.
The enemy finally caught up with her on 13th November 1941 when
U-81 obtained a single torpedo hit on the carrier's starboard side. The
ship was less than 50 miles from Gibraltar at the time of the attack but
despite all-night efforts to tow her to harbour she was lost at about
dawn on the following day, within sight of the Rock of Gibraltar. Poor
damage control procedures had contributed to her loss but only one
man lost his life and sufficient aircraft were airborne at the time of the
torpedoing to be able to maintain two squadrons, one of Swordfish, and
one of Fulmars, at Gibraltar for nearly six months after their parent
ship had sunk.

U-boats were at this time passing into the Mediterranean on the
surface at night. The small RAF unit at Gibraltar had no radar-
equipped search aircraft to block the Straits and it fell to 812 Squadron,
with the Air to Surface Vessel radar to fulfil this vital task; despite a
shortage of radar spares this squadron flew 300 hours on night searches
in the Straits between 30th November and 21st December 1941. In
the course of the three weeks five U-boats were damaged and forced to
return to their Atlantic bases and on the night of 21st/22nd December
the squadrons efforts were crowned with success when U-451 was sunk
by depth-charge attack off Tangier, the first submarine to be sunk at
night by an aircraft. The Fulmars of 807 Squadron meanwhile flew
day A/S patrols and although they made several attacks their inadequate
offensive capacity proved to be more damaging to the enemy's morale
than to the structure of the U-boats. The overall effect of the tenacious
manner in which the Fleet Air Arm held the Straits by day and night
dissuaded the enemy from attempting the passage again until the following
Spring.

THE WESTERN MEDITERRANEAN

January 1942 to October 1942

After the loss of ARK ROYAL the only carrier available was ARGUS; as she was too slow and small for efficient operations with Force H, her only operations were brief sorties in the western Mediterranean, seldom far from Gibraltar, with a handful of Swordfish of 812 Squadron and Fulmars from 807 at Gibraltar embarked. Owing to the general shortage of carriers no Fleet unit could be spared, even for Force H. With the outbreak of War in the Far East in December 1941 INDOMITABLE, the newest of the armoured carriers, was earmarked for that area; ILLUSTRIOUS and FORMIDABLE were just finishing repairs in the United States, while VICTORIOUS was fully committed with the Home Fleet. Of the older ships, only EAGLE was near completing a re-fit, FURIOUS being in the United States for her first extensive re-fit since the beginning of the War.

EAGLE joined Force H in March 1942, ARGUS remaining to provide a spare deck. Shortage of fighters was the principal drawback to operations, EAGLE not having space for more than two Sea Hurricanes in addition to her 18 Swordfish. ARGUS therefore embarked a flight of 807 Squadron's Fulmars when required for ferry operations. The first Spitfires to serve outside the British Isles were flown off to Malta from EAGLE in March 1942, and these sorties continued, until by the end of July 275 Spitfires had been flown off and delivered to the island. The United States Navy carrier WASP made two trips, in April and May; on both occasions 47 Spitfires were flown off by WASP, and on the latter they were joined by another 17 from EAGLE. Out of the 111 aircraft only four failed to reach their destination.

By the beginning of June 1942 Malta's supply position was precarious. For some time the only essential supplies to arrive had been brought by submarines and fast minelayers. A convoy was therefore dispatched from each end of the Mediterranean at the beginning of the second week in June. EAGLE's fighters were reinforced by the addition of 801 Squadron's Sea Hurricanes, at the expense of a Swordfish squadron, and ARGUS again embarked a handful of Fulmars. The western half of the convoy operation was given the heaviest possible protection, but there was no carrier available for the contingent sailing from Alexandria, and the RAF could not spare sufficient long-range fighters to provide adequate cover.

The passage of "Harpoon", as the east-bound convoy was code-named, was contested by all forms of enemy air attack, but at the time of the carriers' detachment on 14th June, as the Sicilian Narrows were approached, only one merchant ship and one destroyer had been sunk by what amounted to a maximum effort on the part of the Axis air forces. Eleven enemy aircraft were destroyed by the Fleet fighters. The convoy continued through the Narrows under cover of darkness, but, on the following day, when within range of the Maltese fighters, three more merchantmen were sunk—all by air attack.

DISPOSITION OF VESSELS AND SQUADRONS

Force H and HARPOON Convoy — 1942
EAGLE — From March 1942
    813 Squadron   9 Swordfish and 2 Sea Hurricanes
    824   ,,   9 Swordfish (not embarked for HARPOON)
    801   ,,   12 Sea Hurricanes (embarked June for HARPOON)
ARGUS
    807 Squadron   6 Fulmars
    824   ,,   4 Swordfish (detachment—remainder of Sqn. at Gibraltar)
Operation PEDESTAL — August 1942
VICTORIOUS (Flagship Rear Admiral Aircraft Carriers — RAdm.A.L.St G. Lyster)
    809 Squadron   12 Fulmars
    884   ,,   6 Fulmars
    885   ,,   6 Sea Hurricanes
    817   ,,   2 Albacores (9 detachment)
    832   ,,   12 Albacores
INDOMITABLE — bombed 12th August 1942
    800 Squadron   12 Sea Hurricanes
    806   ,,   6 Martlet IIs
    880   ,,   12 Sea Hurricanes
    827   ,,   12 Albacores
    831   ,,   12 Albacores
EAGLE — sunk by U-73, 11th August 1942
    801 Squadron   12 Sea Hurricanes
    813   ,,   2 Sea Hurricanes (Swordfish disembarked at Gibraltar)
    824   ,,   9 Swordfish
FURIOUS — ferry and fly off 38 Spitfires to Malta
    804 Squadron   6 Sea Hurricanes
    822   ,,   9 Albacores

The westbound convoy was subjected to continuous air attack, but it was the knowledge that the Italian battlefleet was out that forced Rear Admiral Vian to turn back. With only light cruisers, no air cover, and only 33% AA ammunition remaining the losses incurred in proceeding would have been grievous. As it was two merchant ships and two destroyers were lost to air attack before turning back.

EAGLE flew another 55 Spitfires into Malta in June, and another 59 in July, in the course of four separate operations, but by the end of the latter month there were only 80 fighters left, out of the 275 delivered since March. As they were being written-off at the rate of 17 per week in the course of the enemy air offensive, another ferry sortie was vital. The stores brought in at such cost in June were fast running out, and the arrival of a convoy was essential to the survival of the island.

It was decided that on this occasion there would be only one convoy, from the west, and the operation, "Pedestal", was mounted in the second week in August. The fourteen fast merchantmen had the strongest screen provided for any convoy to date: two battleships, seven cruisers, 20 destroyers and three Fleet carriers. VICTORIOUS had been detached from the Home Fleet, INDOMITABLE from the Eastern Fleet, and, with EAGLE, they boasted of more than 70 Sea Hurricanes, Fulmars, and Martlets, in addition to the Swordfish and Albacores. In the ferry role was FURIOUS, with 38 Spitfires as well as her half-dozen Sea Hurricanes.

The powerful force passed through the Straits of Gibraltar on the night of 9th/10th August 1942 and remained as close to the coast of Algeria as was prudent. "Pedestal" was detected by the enemy early on the 11th and that afternoon, as FURIOUS was flying off the Spitfires, EAGLE was hit by four torpedoes from U-73, and sank in less than eight minutes, some 80 miles north of Algiers. With her fine offensive record, she was a great loss to the Royal Navy: in her last five months of service she had supplied Malta with more than 180 Spitfires. She was the last Fleet carrier to be lost by the Royal Navy during the War.

The expected air attacks began at dusk on 11th, and mounted in intensity during the course of the following day, the enemy throwing their entire offensive weight against the convoy. Throughout the day only one merchant ship was damaged: she straggled and was sunk the next day by air attack, close to the Tunisian coast. The fighters broke up most of the attacks, and the only other ship to be hit while the carriers were with the convoy was VICTORIOUS which took a heavy bomb directly on her flight deck, breaking up on the armour. At dusk however, after the heavy cover had detached at the Sicilian Narrows, the enemy directed a strike of over 100 aircraft at the carriers. The fighters, whittled down to half of their original strength by losses (including all EAGLE'S Sea Hurricanes) and their pilots exhausted by a full day of combat, were overwhelmed. VICTORIOUS came through the attack un-scathed but INDOMITABLE was hit on her flight deck by two armour-piercing bombs, fore and aft, and another very near-miss blew in a 30 ft underwater hole aft. Again the armour deck saved the carrier from destruction, but again the damage necessitated repairs in the United States and the ship being out of action for months.

Thirty enemy aircraft were shot down—five by Lieutenant R. J. Cork DSC RNVR, who flew four sorties on 12th August in the only Sea Hurricane IC aboard INDOM. 13 Fleet fighters were lost, in addition to the aircraft lost aboard EAGLE and INDOMITABLE.

The convoy, still 13 strong, pressed on escorted by four cruisers and twelve destroyers. During the night of 12th/13th Italian MAS-boats (MTBs) sank four merchant ships and the cruiser MANCHESTER; U-boats accounted for the much-needed AA cruiser CAIRO and dam-aged the other two cruisers. Enemy aircraft took up the attack at daybreak on 13th, and another four merchantmen were sunk, well within effective fighter range of Malta. Five ships finally entered Grand Harbour, at least two in a sinking condition, and unloaded 32,000 tons of stores. With the petroleum from the OHIO, the fate of Malta was assured.

The losses inflicted on the enemy in the course of the convoy battle and the increased RAF fighter strength in Malta prevented the enemy from mounting air attacks on the scale possible before August 1942. FURIOUS flew off another 32 Spitfires at the end of August. The enemy air offensive had fallen off to such an extent after this operation that only one further ferry trip was required, when FURIOUS delivered the last 29 Spitfires for Malta, in mid-October 1942.

Malta's survival was assured by the perseverance of the Royal Navy, which incurred severe losses in the process. This in no way belittles the magnificent fight put up by the defenders: without the Navy the supplies would not have reached the island, and there would have been nothing with which to fight. The fate of the eastern convoy in the June 1942 operation underlines the vital part played by the aircraft carriers.

828 and 830 Squadrons

The main weight of the offensive against the Axis lines of communications between Europe and N. Africa was taken by Malta. The greatest proportion of the enemy tonnage sunk, some 45%, was claimed by the island-based submarines, while the aircraft came after with 37% of the total. Under the direction of the RAF AoC, shipping strike became a joint service undertaking: reconnaissance aircraft detected enemy movements by day; the Swordfish and Albacores illuminated the shipping for their own torpedoes, and for those of RAF Wellingtons; on the following day the scattered survivors were attacked by Blenheims and torpedo-carrying Beauforts. Although there were seldom more than four or five naval Torpedo Spotter Reconnaissance aircraft available for any strike, the two squadrons sank over 30 ships and damaged another 50, the sinkings representing 11% of the total of enemy ships lost to all causes.

When no Axis shipping presented itself, night strikes were flown against factories, airfields and harbours in Sicily and Calabria. The sum of all these operations resulted in a high rate of attrition and 830 was absorbed by 828 Squadron towards the end of 1942. Operations continued until the end of the campaign in Tunisia, in May 1943, with the squadron flying from bases in North Africa as well as Malta, principally on anti-submarine patrols.

AMPHIBIOUS OPERATIONS IN THE MEDITERRANEAN—
November 1942 to October 1944:
Operation "Torch"

After the "Pedestal" convoy operation in August 1942 there was little carrier activity in the Mediterranean. FURIOUS remained with Force H, taking part in two ferry operations (August and October). No other carrier was available—INDOMITABLE was repairing action damage, VICTORIOUS had returned to the Home Fleet for a short re-fit and covering operations for the September Arctic convoy, PQ18/QP14. EAGLE had been lost but her surviving Swordfish squadron, 813, which had been left behind at Gibraltar to make space for Sea Hurricanes, remained on the Rock for local patrols. The Swordfish remained in the theatre of operations until the end of 1943, providing A/S cover for the mass of shipping involved in the invasion of North Africa, and subsequently from Algerian airfields. The squadron returned to Britain where they embarked for a highly successful commission in CAMPANIA, escorting convoys until the end of the War.

DISPOSITION OF VESSELS AND SQUADRONS

Operation TORCH — The Invasion of North Africa — November 1942
Force H — Covering Group:
FORMIDABLE

885 Squadron	6 Seafires	
888 "	6 Martlets	
893 "	18 Martlets and Fulmars	
820 "	12 Albacores	

VICTORIOUS

809 Squadron	12 Fulmars
882 "	12 Martlets
884 "	6 Fulmars
817 "	9 Albacores
832 "	8 Albacores (B Flight disembarked at Manston)

Centre Naval Task Group: **Oran:**
FURIOUS — detached from Covering Group at midnight 7/8th November

801 Squadron	10 Seafires
807 "	10 Seafires
822 "	8 Albacores (C Flight disembarked at Gibraltar)

BITER

800 Squadron	15 Sea Hurricanes
833 "	3 Swordfish (disembarked at Gibraltar, returned in ARGUS)

DASHER

804 Squadron	6 Sea Hurricanes
891 "	9 Sea Hurricanes

Eastern Naval Task Force — **Algiers:**
ARGUS

880 Squadron	12 Seafires

AVENGER — torpedoed and sunk by U-155 on 15 th November

802 Squadron	9 Sea Hurricanes
883 "	6 Sea Hurricanes

Operation TORCH — The American Carriers off the Moroccan Coast
Northern Attack Group — Port Lyautey:
SANGAMON

Auxiliary Fighter Squadron	26 (VGF 26)	12 Wildcats
Auxiliary Scouting Squadron	26 (VGS 26)	9 Avengers and 9 Dauntlesses

CHENANGO — Ferrying 76 USAAF P-40F (Warhawks)
Centre Attack Group — Casablanca/Fedhala:
RANGER

Fighter Squadron	9 (VF 9)	27 Wildcats
Fighter Squadron	41 (VF 41)	27 Wildcats
Scouting Squadron	41 (VS 41)	18 Dauntlesses
Commander Air Group	9	1 Avenger

SUWANEE

VGF 27	11 Wildcats
VGF 28	12 Wildcats (lent from CHENANGO)
VGS 30	6 Wildcats (Fighter Flight from CHARGER)
VGS 27	9 Avengers

Southern Attack Group — Safi:
SANTEE

VGF 29	14 Wildcats
VGS 29	8 Avengers and 9 Dauntlesses

With the safety of Malta assured, the Royal Navy was able to commence detailed planning for the first major Allied amphibious landings. Vichy Morocco and Algeria where chosen as the first objectives—targets were less heavily defended and many of the defenders were thought to be sympathetic to the Allied cause. With the El Alamein offensive under way the vast pincer movement was intended to place the entire southern shore of the Mediterranean in Allied hands.

Force H was reinforced from the Home Fleet, new construction and the Eastern Fleet. No less than 130 fighters were embarked in seven carriers together with 30-odd torpedo-bombers, these embarked in the three Fleet carriers. The Royal Navy was to provide air cover and close support for the landings at Oran and Algiers, until such time as the nearby airfields fell into the hands of the ground forces, when RAF and USAAF aircraft positioned at Gibraltar would be flown in. The landings on the Moroccan coast were wholly an American commitment, air cover being provided by 136 naval aircraft from four US Navy carriers. The overall operation was code-named "Torch".

The British movements commenced on 22nd October 1942, when AVENGER left Loch Ewe with the slow military convoy KMS1, and BITER sailed with the fast counterpart, KMF1, from the Clyde. The remaining carriers proceeded in completely military formations. All the escort carriers, two taking part in their first operation, had embarked three Swordfish for A/S protection on passage. On arrival at Gibraltar the Swordfish were disembarked, and the A/S task was undertaken by Albacores from the fleet carriers, supported by RAF Hudsons.

Although the Axis sighted a few of the many formations en route, no ships were lost before the landings, which came off just before midnight on 7th/8th November. The airfields in the Algiers sector were captured at an early stage, one by an American Regimental Combat Team and the other, Blida, by the Martlets of 882 Squadron. The leader of a patrol had seen white flags on the airfield and, covered by the other aircraft of his flight, had landed to take the surrender of the commandant. The airfield was held by the squadron until mid-morning (8th) when a Commando arrived to take over on a more permanent basis. All carriers had flown aircraft on the dawn strike against coastal defences and the airfields, and with the assistance of the land-based Air Forces, which had first landed at Algiers/Maison Blanche at 0900 on 8th, they made a large contribution to the swift end of resistance in the area, which was in Allied hands by nightfall, less than 24 hours after the first landings.

Oran was a far more difficult proposition: memories of the Royal Navy's attacks in July 1940 were very bitter and therefore American ground forces were exclusively employed, whereas Algiers had been a joint operation. Initial air cover was provided entirely by the Fleet Air Arm, many of whose aircraft sported a plain white star instead of the standard roundel, but this was as much to protect the aircraft from "friendly" ground-fire, there being the possibility that the Americans might have confused the British markings with the tricouleur, as much as to deceive the Vichy French defenders.

FURIOUS' aircraft took most of the weight of the first dawn strike on the airfields. In one spectacularly successful attack on La Senia the Albacores and Seafires destroyed 47 enemy aircraft on the ground. Losses were heavy—five of the eight Albacores were lost, together with at least one Seafire, all to the heavy flak. Tafaroui, the other airfield in the vicinity, was also bombed and strafed, and in the two strikes over 80% of the serviceable Vichy aircraft in the Oran sector were destroyed on the ground. A few air combats took place, in which the opposing Dewoitine 520s were quickly disposed of—one such combat resulting in the first victory for the Seafire, in action for the first time.

The Sea Hurricanes from the escort carriers concentrated on providing the troops with close air cover, the aircraft of BITER's 800 Squadron claiming no fewer than five D. 520s while covering American troops south of Oran. Tactical reconnaissance was provided by Fulmars from VICTORIOUS. Both types had considerably success in their roles, to which a great deal of training had been devoted during the preceeding months while the squadrons had been working-up ashore in the United Kingdom. Unfortunately DASHER's 804 Squadron, also operating in the Oran area, was unable to find the carrier on return and all the Sea Hurricanes forced-landed in American-held territory.

The carriers continued to give support to the operations until 10th November, by which time the Air Forces were fully operational ashore, and fighting with Vichy forces was ended. The fleet carriers, VICTORIOUS and FORMIDABLE, had covered the inshore escort carrier squadrons, ARGUS and AVENGER at Algiers and FURIOUS, BITER and DASHER at Oran, not only from air attack, but also from a possible excursion by the Italian battlefleet, still a power to be reckoned with. As soon as it became apparent that there was little risk of inter-ference from the latter direction the Albacores were freed for full-scale attacks on enemy defensive positions ashore. The quick end to the fighting at the entrance to Algiers harbour was due in large measure to the effectiveness of the dive-bombing by the naval squadrons. In addition to these planned strikes, the Albacores gave on-request support to the troops, and provided close A/S patrols around the shipping inshore.

The escort carriers covered returning convoys during their withdrawal, and it was while escorting MKF1 that AVENGER was torpedoed by U-155 on 15th November. Only one torpedo hit, but the ship did not have the modifications incorporated in later escort carriers, and she blew up, leaving only 17 survivors. Some retribution was later exacted by FORMIDABLE and VICTORIOUS. The former also avenged the battleship BARHAM, an Albacore of 820 torpedoing U-331, which had been previously attacked by a naval Walrus and Hudsons.

VICTORIOUS' success came four days later, on 21st November, when one of her Albacores found and depth-charged U-517 in mid-Atlantic.

Operation "Torch" provided invaluable experience for the subsequent amphibious operations, both in the Mediterranean and in the Pacific. A clear indication was given that carrier aircraft could provide air cover for an opposed landing until land-based aircraft could be brought into action from captured airfields. Off North Africa the carriers had the task for only a few hours; later operations which involved more extensive support over longer periods proved the feasibility and indeed the necessity for strong carrier forces.

Force H 1943—Operation "Husky"

FURIOUS and FORMIDABLE remained with Force H after the departure of the smaller carriers from the North African beach-heads. With a powerful Italian battlefleet still in commission there was always the definite threat of a break-out from La Spezia, the obvious objective of which would be the vast amount of Allied shipping supplying the Allied armies in North Africa. FURIOUS left for the Home Fleet in January 1943, to replace VICTORIOUS, lent to the United States Navy for operations in the South West Pacific. By this time the immediate danger from surface intervention was lessened and FORMIDABLE, backed by NELSON and RODNEY, remained as the only aircraft carrier in the Mediterranean.

Force H was based on Oran for the majority of the time, but it spent a few weeks at Gibraltar from mid-March after the battlecriuser SCHARNHORST was moved from the Baltic to join an already powerful

---

DISPOSITION OF VESSELS AND SQUADRONS

Operation HUSKY — July 1943
INDOMITABLE — damaged by air torpedoes 11th July

807 Squadron	10	Seafires
880 ,,	10	Seafires
899 ,,	10	Seafires
817 ,,	21	Albacores

FORMIDABLE

885 Squadron	6	Seafires
888 ,,	8	Martlets
893 ,,	12	Martlets
820 ,,	18	Albacores

Operation AVALANCHE — 9th to 12th September 1943
Force H (9th to 11th)
ILLUSTRIOUS — Flag Rear Admiral C. Moody RN

878 Squadron	12	Martlets
890 ,,	8	Martlets
894 ,,	9	Seafires (6 a/c to Paestum via UNICORN)
810 ,,	12	Barracudas

FORMIDABLE
Aircraft complement as in HUSKY
Force V — Flag Rear Admiral Sir Philip Vian RN in EURYALUS
ATTACKER

879 Squadron	10	Seafires
886 ,,	10	Seafires

BATTLER

807 Squadron	12	Seafires
808 ,,	9	Seafires

HUNTER

834 Squadron	6	Seafires (Fighter Flight)
899 ,,	12	Seafires

STALKER

880 Squadron	18	Seafires

UNICORN

809 Squadron	10	Seafires
887 ,,	10	Seafires
897 ,,	10	Seafires
894 ,,	6	Seafires (detached from ILLUSTRIOUS 11th September)

naval squadron in northern Norway; Force H was retained as a reserve against a possible break-out by any or all of these ships. Occasionally FORMIDABLE's squadrons were disembarked to operate from shore bases, to fly local patrols or provide fighter defence of the Oran area. The carrier herself was unserviceable at the time of the end of the Tunisian campaign, with her fighters at Gibraltar while 820's Albacores joined Desert Air Force Wellingtons at Böne to form a night-shipping strike force, to cover the light forces engaged in shooting-up the retreating Axis forces off Cap Bon, against the Italian Fleet.

After the termination of the Tunisian campaign in early May 1943, the next landings were planned to go ashore in Sicily. With sufficient airfields available in Malta and Tunisia to provide all the needs of the amphibious forces the carriers were not required in the close support role but rather in the traditional role of Force H—heavy cover in the event of an Italian Navy intervention.

FORMIDABLE was joined by the recently repaired INDOMITABLE and the Force was stationed some 180 miles to the east of Malta. This position was well clear of the invasion area, but only a few hours steaming distant: an initial sighting of the Italian fleet, which still possessed six battleships, seven cruisers and 48 destroyers, could swiftly be followed by a day or night torpedo strike by the forty-odd Albacores embarked in the two ships. In spite of the fact that this was the first Allied landing on the shores of metropolitan Italy, the Italian fleet was so cowed that they made no attempt to interfere and the carrier aircraft flew only patrols for the protection of the Force and nearby naval units. The landings commenced on 10th July 1943, and the main enemy reaction came in the form of air attack on the shipping to the south of Sicily. On the evening of 11th, however, a solitary Ju 88 torpedo-bomber surprised the carriers and put a torpedo into INDOMITABLE's port side, causing extensive damage to the adjacent boiler-room; the aircraft escaped without a shot being fired in return. INDOM. was taking part in her first operation since the damage received in the previous August, and she was put out of action again for nearly a year.

With Sicily securely in Allied hands, FORMIDABLE entered Grand Harbour, the first carrier to do so since ILLUSTRIOUS had sought refuge for repairs after her bombing in January 1941. The occasion was symbolic—no other aircraft carrier was to be damaged by enemy air attack in the Mediterranean.

Landings in Italy quickly followed the reduction of Sicily, the first foothold being in Calabria. Although the advance from Reggio was going well, it was decided that a landing in the Bay of Salerno would lead to the swift capture of the well-equipped port of Naples and to the blocking of the Axis retreat from the South. The planned assault area was so far from the airfields in Malta and Sicily that the use of carrier aircraft for initial cover was essential; although the Allied Air Forces in the Mediterranean possessed nearly 4,000 aircraft of all types, the distance involved in the operation meant that only 36 aircraft from Sicilian bases could be over the beach-head at any one time, and that they would only be able to remain on call for 20 minutes at a time.

Martlet IIIs of 805 Squadron take off from Mersa Matruh while operating as a component of the Royal Naval Fighter Squadron in late 1941. "A" is AX728, an ex-US Navy, ex-Greek F4F-3A
[*IWM*

Caudron Luciolles aboard ARK ROYAL prior to flying Free French personnel ashore to negotiate terms for the surrender of Dakar (23rd September, 1940)   [*via Lt Cdr R. B. M. Wilkins, RN*

A Swordfish of 810 Squadron leaves ARK ROYAL's starboard catapult as a Skua of 803 Squadron
is readied on the port catapult trolley.   Few photographs exist of Swordfish catapult launches
[Lt Cdr F. J. Dodd

"G"—L2889 of 800 Squadron being extricated from ARK's barrier.   Note the extended dive-
brakes and the ventral recess and ejector yoke for the single 250lb or 500lb bomb
[via J. D. Brown

A Swordfish of 818 Squadron misses ARK ROYAL's arrester wires and is photographed at the moment of entry into the barrier; the drum aft of the pilot is the long-tange fuel tank, occupying what was normally the observer's cockpit   [*Lt Cdr F. J. Dodd*

Hurricane Z3061 is loaded aboard ARK ROYAL at Gibraltar: March 1941

[*via FAA Museum*

Eight of the dozen RAF Hurricanes launched from ARK for Malta on 2nd April 1941
[via FAA Museum

Fulmars of 808 Squadron and Skuas of 800 Squadron launching from ARK ROYAL. The chockmen are just clearing the first Fulmar in the range, and the presence of two more chockmen on the
starboard side of the deck indicates that two aircraft have already flown off   [IWM

Fulmars at readiness aft as ARK ROYAL escorts a Malta convoy in November 1941—Operation "Halberd". In the background is the cruiser KENYA   [*IWM*

7B of 808 Squadron taking off for a fighter patrol   [*Lt Cdr P. J. Spelling*

Another Fulmar of 807 in the process of a non-standard overshoot, while the batsman escapes
up the deck   [*IWM*

ARGUS, ARK ROYAL and MALAYA returning from ARK's last operation : November 13th 1941
                                                                                [*A. J. Ward*

ARK ROYAL immediately after being torpedoed by U-81. She is still making about 12 knots
and has already taken up a considerable list to starboard   [*A. J. Ward*

January 1942: ARGUS turns into wind to launch two Fulmars of 807 Squadron off the Spanish
coast   [*IWM*

A Spitfire V is readied for flying off from EAGLE to Malta. Ranged on the starboard deck edge are the Sea Hurricanes of 813 Squadron's fighter flight. The containers beneath the Spitfire's port wing-tip are shell drums for the 20mm cannon   [/WM

INDOMITABLE at Freetown en route from the Indian Ocean to join the heavy escort for Operation "Pedestal". 880 Squadron's Sea Hurricane IBs are identifiable by the white band on the engine cowling, immediately aft of the spinner, while 800's aircraft have a white band around the after fuselage. In addition, the numeral 6 is omitted from the fuselage code-number on 880's aircraft, while the numeral 7 is retained on 800's. Also on deck are four Martlet IIs of 806 Squadron and four Albacores of 827 and 831 Squadrons   [/WM

10th August 1942: one of the last photographs of EAGLE, seen here astern of INDOMITABLE in the Western Mediterranean.   Note that INDOMITABLE is carrying at least one Swordfish (starboard side) although she normally embarked only Albacores   [IWM

An Albacore of FORMIDABLE's 820 Squadron is armed with six 250lb bombs in preparation for a strike on the Algiers area.   The tip of the white star which replaced the roundels for "Torch" can be seen between the tails of the inboard and centre bombs; the Seafire IB of 885 Squadron in the background also bears the star beneath its starboard wing-tip   [IWM

FN 121 (9-Z), a Martlet IV of 893 Squadron takes off from FORMIDABLE in support of the
North African landings   [IWM

BITER (800 Sqdn) and AVENGER (802 and 883 Sqdns) returning from their stations off Oran
and Algiers.   A few days later, on 15th November 1942, AVENGER (*left*) was sunk by U-155.
The permanent deck park of six Sea Hurricanes in each ship was necessitated by the lack of
wing-folding in this type of aircraft.   [IWM

FORMIDABLE en route for Salerno—September 1943.   The positions of the out-rigger stowages for the Seafire IICs are well-illustrated.   Seven of the 18 Martlet IVs of 888 and 893 Squadrons are ranged on deck   [*IWM*

FORMIDABLE off Gibraltar—Spring 1943.   Both Seafire IBs are parked on outriggers, with only the forward end of the aircraft over the deck.   The aircraft remained on deck at all times, and the resulting loss of finish on the alloy engine cowlings is self-evident   [*IWM*

Dawn, 15th August 1944: Task Force 88 off the French Riveria, PURSUER leading ATTACKER
and KHEDIVE   [D. J. Frearson

Wildcat VIs of 881 Squadron take off in support of the "Dragoon" landings   [D. J. Frearson

Bombing up 881's Wildcats with 250 pounders   [*D. J. Frearson*

A Seafire III of KHEDIVE's 899 Squadron takes off for a dive-bombing attack on German positions in the South of France   [*MoD (Admiralty)*]

Task Force 88 returns from "Dragoon" through the Straits of Messina: 21st August 1944
[*MoD* (*Admiralty*)]

18 of 899's Seafire IIIs ranged on KHEDIVE between "Dragoon" and the mopping-up operations in the Aegean; the ship is in Parlatorio Creek, Grand Harbour
[*MoD* (*Admiralty*)]

879 Squadron prepares to launch from ATTACKER in the Aegean. At least three of the Seafire IIIs are armed with a single 500lb bomb apiece   [*IWM*

HUNTER (807 Sqdn) refuels an escort during Aegean operations to the north of Crete in September 1944   [*IWM*

INDOMITABLE en route for Aden to embark Hurricanes for Ceylon. Four of 880 Squadron's
Sea Hurricanes are on deck, three on outriggers   [IWM

Martlet II AM977, "A" of 888 Squadron, is launched from FORMIDABLE in the Indian Ocean.
The parellel bars on the deck, on either side of the catapult track, were used to align the aircraft
with the catapult   [IWM

main Fleet base in Ceylon, on 2nd April after exercising en route. The succeeding fortnight was spent in careful planning and rehearsal for a strike on Sabang, a harbour at the northern extremity of Sumatra.

The 27 warships of six Allied Navies sailed from Trincomalee on 16th April 1944 and after refuelling arrived at the launch position, some 100 miles south-west of Sabang Island, in the early hours of 19th. ILLUSTRIOUS launched 17 Barracudas and 13 Corsairs, while the larger SARATOGA provided 11 Avengers, 18 Dauntlesses and 24 Hellcats. The aircraft delivered a highly co-ordinated strike which was opposed only by flak, the latter only opening fire after the attack was well under way. There was little shipping present in the harbour, but one small freighter was sunk and another damaged and driven aground; oil storage tanks were destroyed and heavy damage inflicted upon the port facilities. In a suppressive sweep over the airfields, the Corsair and Hellcats destroyed 24 enemy aircraft on the ground. Only one aircraft, a Hellcat, was lost from the strike, and the pilot was rescued by an RN submarine stationed off the coast for that purpose. Not until the Fleet withdrew did the Japanese attempt to attack the Fleet, but the three G4M torpedo bombers were quickly "splashed" by Hellcats of the Combat Air Patrol.

On return to Trinco SARATOGA was ordered to return to the United States for a refit and it was decided to combine her eastward passage with a strike on the important aviation fuel store at Soerabaya (Surabaja) in Java. As the target was closer to Western Australia than to Ceylon the Fleet staged through Exmouth Gulf to re-fuel before arriving at the flying-off position some 180 miles south of Soerabaya just after daybreak on 17th May 1944. ILLUSTRIOUS' Barracudas had given way to Avengers as the distance to the target (across the breadth of Java) was too great for the Barra. The strike consisted of 45 Avengers and Dauntlesses, escorted by 40 Corsairs and Hellcats, attacking in two waves. One struck at the refinery while the other went for the dockyard and shipping in the harbour. Surprise was again achieved, but the results were slender. One small ship (1,000 grt) was sunk and little damage was done to the refinery. Fortunately only one aircraft was lost.

The lack of success enjoyed by the strikes became evident at the debriefing, but, following the then-current Royal Navy practice, the C-in-C was aboard a capital ship rather than a carrier, and it was not until the carriers had withdrawn far enough for a restrike to be impracticable that Somerville learnt of the disappointing results. The Fleet split up shortly after the withdrawal began, SARATOGA and her three destroyers returning to Pearl Harbour while the other ships returned to Trincomalee.

ILLUSTRIOUS' next operation was a raid on the Andaman Islands on 22nd June 1944. It was her first and only solo operation in this phase, and owing to bad weather in the target area the Barracudas had little success against the few targets available. Several Japanese aircraft were destroyed by strafing on the airfield at Port Blair, and a few small coastal vessels were sunk by the dive-bombers. Lack of adequate intelligence robbed many of the strikes of this period of the force which they might otherwise have had, while overt reconnaissance would have alerted the enemy to the likelihood of imminent carrier strikes.

In early July, the Eastern Fleet was reinforced by the arrival of VICTORIOUS, fresh from her Norwegian strikes, and INDOMITABLE, recently returned to service after the torpedo damage incurred off Sicily a year before. VICTORIOUS joined ILLUSTRIOUS in what proved to be Admiral Somerville's last operation prior to relief by Admiral Sir Bruce Fraser. This operation was a bombardment of Sabang, the target of the April strike. To provide full defensive cover for the attack ILLUSTRIOUS landed most of her Barracudas and replaced them with an additional fighter squadron, giving her 42 Corsairs, while VIC embarked her normal complement of 28 Corsairs and 21 Barracudas.

In addition to bombardment spotting, provided by the Corsairs, the carrier aircraft struck at shipping in the harbour, shore installations and airfields. The bombardment by three battleships, seven cruisers and two destroyers was extremely effective, while the air strikes again destroyed the oil storage tanks burnt out during the previous strike, but which had since been repaired. Again there was little shipping in the harbour, and only two small ships, totalling 1,500 tons, were sunk. Only superficial damage was inflicted on the bombarding ships, and no aircraft were lost, while the Fleet CAP shot down four enemy aircraft and sweeps over the airfields accounted for another two.

After the Sabang bombardment ILLUSTRIOUS proceeded to South Africa for a short refit, her first for over a year, and Rear Admiral C. Moody, Rear Admiral, Aircraft Carrier Squadron, took INDOMITABLE and VICTORIOUS to strike at Sumatran targets, the cement works at Indaroeng and the harbour at Emmahaven. The Barracuda attack on the cement works, the largest in South East Asia, was successful, reducing the output for several months; the strike on the port and shipping was less successful, only two ships, totalling 6,000 tons, were damaged. No enemy air opposition was encountered, and the Fleet Air Arm's losses were negligible. This operation, at the end of August 1944, was followed up with a strike, by the same ships, on the important rail centre of Sigli in northern Sumatra on 18th September. Although a fair amount of damage was done, neither Rear Admiral Moody nor Admiral Fraser were impressed with the performance of their offensive force, and an extensive training programme was initiated to raise the standard of weaponry in the strike squadrons. To be fair to the aircrew, they had suffered from lack of up-to-date knowledge of the target areas, which were at the extreme limit of the coverage of the limited long-range reconnaissance aircraft available in India at the time.

The next offensive operation by the carrier squadron was in the nature of diversionary support for the American forces about to commence the landings in Leyte Gulf. In an attempt to draw off Japanese naval forces, INDOMITABLE and VICTORIOUS struck at the Nicobar Islands for the three days preceding the assault on Leyte, simulating a pre-invasion bombardment. The enemy was fully pre-occupied with the impending events in the Phillippines, some 2,000 miles to the east, and there was no obvious reaction to the diversion. The targets were

again few and far between, although there were enemy fighters encountered for the first time since the bombardment of Sabang. Half a dozen
Ki 43 fighters were shot down by the Hellcats and Corsairs, at no loss
to the Fleet Air Arm aircraft, giving the former type their first victories
in the East Indies. The Barracudas sank a considerable number of small
craft and coasters, for the loss of only one aircraft to ground-fire. The
strikes, which went on for three days, from 17th to 19th October 1944,
were the first in which the Allied force had remained in the combat
area for more than a matter of hours. The immunity enjoyed by the
Fleet, coupled with the loss of only two aircraft in three days (the other
loss was on take-off) gave immeasurable confidence as to the possibilities of the carrier strike force to the personnel concerned. Underway
replenishment was practiced by all the ships, as a vital preparation for
the forthcoming operations in Pacific waters.

Nearly two months elapsed before the Carrier Squadron undertook
another operation. The intervening time was taken up with intensive
weapons training and working up with the Avengers which replaced the
Barracudas after the Nicobars operation. ILLUSTRIOUS rejoined the
Fleet, and INDEFATIGABLE joined from the Home Fleet, embarking
between them some 120 Corsairs, Avengers, Seafires and Fireflies.

To a formidable carrier force was added a formidable commander
in the person of Sir Philip Vian, who had commanded the escort carriers
off Salerno, after a brilliant career in destroyers and cruisers.

Unfortunately the first operation under Rear Admiral Vian proved
abortive due to bad weather; a strike force of 27 Avengers and 28 Corsairs
and Hellcats which had set out for the refinery at Pangkalan Brandon
in Sumatra, on 20th December 1944, being forced to strike at the secondary target instead. The latter, the port of Belawan Deli, near Medan,
was obscured by low cloud and heavy squalls, and the strike achieved
only modest results. No aircraft were lost, and as the Fleet withdrew,
fighters attacked the airfields in the vicinity of Sabang, destroying
several Japanese aircraft on the ground.

After returning to Trincomalee, Vian stayed long enough to add
INDEFAT. to his strength before sortie-ing once again for a re-strike
on Pangkalan Brandon. The combined Air Groups attacked on 4th
January 1945, Avengers and Fireflies bombing and rocketing, while
Corsairs and Hellcats carried out a sweep over enemy airfields before
the strike, as well as providing close escort for the strike aircraft. The
strike, executed in good weather, was a complete success. Heavy
damage was inflicted on the refinery, considerably reducing the output,
while the fighters destroyed about a dozen enemy aircraft in air combat,
and another 20 of all types in strafing attacks on the airfields. The
cost to the strike was one Avenger, the crew being rescued. This operation was conducted by the last Fleet carrier force to sortie from and return
to Trincomalee—Scapa Flow in Technicolor, as it was known to the
thousands of men with the Eastern Fleet.

By the end of 1944 agreement had at last been reached as to the conditions of employment for the British Pacific Fleet in what had been
hitherto an exclusively American operational area. Accordingly, the

DISPOSITION OF VESSELS AND SQUADRONS

Sabang (April) and Soerabaya (May) 1944
ILLUSTRIOUS (Barracudas for Sabang, Avengers for Soerabaya, strikes)
1830 Squadron	14 Corsairs	
1833 "	14 Corsairs	
810 "	12 Barracudas—replaced by 832 Squadron—12 Avengers	
847 "	9 Barracudas—replaced by 845 Squadron—12 Avengers	

SARATOGA
VF 12	26 F6F-3 Hellcats
VB 12	24 SBD-5 Dauntlesses
VT 12	18 TBF-1 Avengers
Air Group Leader	1 F6F-3

Andamans Strike — 22nd June 1944
ILLUSTRIOUS — complement as Sabang strike

Bombardment of Sabang — 25th July 1944
ILLUSTRIOUS
1830 Squadron	14 Corsairs
1833 "	14 Corsairs
1837 "	14 Corsairs

VICTORIOUS
1834 Squadron	14 Corsairs
1836 "	14 Corsairs
831 "	21 Barracudas

Emmahaven and Indaroeng Strike — 29th August 1944
VICTORIOUS
1834 Squadron	14 Corsairs (top cover Emmahaven)
1836 "	14 Corsairs (top cover Indaroeng)
831 "	21 Barracudas (both targets)

INDOMITABLE — Flag Rear Admiral C. Moody RN
1839 Squadron	10 Hellcats
1844 "	10 Hellcats
815 "	12 Barracudas (Emmahaven)
817 "	12 Barracudas (Indaroeng)

Sigli Strike — 18th September 1944
VICTORIOUS
1834 Squadron	14 Corsairs
1836 "	14 Corsairs
822 "	21 Barracudas

INDOMITABLE — complement as Emmahaven/Indaroeng strike

Strikes on Nicobar Is. 17th to 19th October 1944
VICTORIOUS
1834 Squadron	14 Corsairs
1836 "	14 Corsairs
831 "	21 Barracudas

INDOMITABLE
1839 Squadron	14 Hellcats
1844 "	14 Hellcats
815 "	12 Barracudas
817 "	12 Barracudas

Belawan Deli — 21st December 1944
ILLUSTRIOUS
1830 Squadron	14 Corsairs
1833 "	14 Corsairs
854 "	21 Avengers

INDOMITABLE — Flag Rear Admiral Vian
1839 Squadron	14 Hellcats
1844 "	14 Hellcats
857 "	21 Avengers

DISPOSITION—continued

PANGKALAN BRANDON — re-strike 4th January 1945
INDOMITABLE — unchanged aircraft complement
VICTORIOUS

1834 Squadron	14 Corsairs
1836 ,,	14 Corsairs
849 ,,	21 Avengers

INDEFATIGABLE

888 Squadron	8 Hellcats (PR detachment)
887 ,,	16 Seafire 111s
894 ,,	16 Seafire 111s
1770 ,,	12 Fireflies
820 ,,	21 Avengers

main striking force of the Eastern Fleet was re-designated and on 16th January 1945 INDEFATIGABLE, INDOMITABLE, VICTORIOUS, ILLUSTRIOUS, KING GEORGE V, three cruisers and 10 destroyers left Ceylon for Sydney, to strike at the oil installations at Palembang en route.

The East Indies Fleet in 1945

With the departure of the British Pacific Fleet in January 1945, only three operational escort carriers were available for duties with a reduced battle-squadron, which comprised QUEEN ELIZABETH, RENOWN, and the French RICHELIEU. The only Assault CVE was AMEER, the others being EMPRESS and SHAH, both armed with Avengers and a Wildcat fighter flight; these fighter flights saw no combat in 1945, as the trade protection ships usually embarked flights or squadrons of Hellcats for specific operations. EMPEROR, HUNTER, KHEDIVE, STALKER and ATTACKER were all earmarked for the 21st Aircraft Carrier Squadron, the air component of the East Indies Fleet, but did not leave the Mediterranean until the end of 1944, becoming operational in the Bay of Bengal from the end of March 1945.

The primary role of the East Indies Fleet was the offshore support of the Fourteenth Army in Burma; a subsidiary role was to contain the single cruiser division which the Japanese maintained at Singapore. The remainder of the Imperial Japanese Navy's strength was in home waters—what was left of it after the Battles of the Philippine Sea, Surigao Strait, and Cape Engano, and the depradations of the USN submarines.

The first operation undertaken by a CVE after Vice Admiral Sir Arthur Power had taken command of the East Indies Fleet in January 1945 was in support of landings on Ramree Island, one of the operations supplementary to the assault on Akyab. AMEER's Hellcats provided Combat Air Patrol over the bombarding QUEEN ELIZABETH and PHOEBE, while the Far East Air Force gave the landing forces close support. After this operation, on 21st January, AMEER went on to supply all the air cover for a Royal Marines landing on Cheduba Island on 26th, dive-bombing and strafing enemy defensive positions. Meanwhile the Japanese defenders on Ramree were fighting stubbornly and to hasten the full occupation of the island landings were made in the south, covered by AMEER.   The Hellcats again attacked enemy positions ashore, greatly assisting the troops in their advance.

After the vital base of Akyab had been secured, XIV Army's main preoccupation was with the break-out from the Imphal Plain, well inland, and the subsequent drive on Mandalay, and such small amphibious operations as were carried out on the Arakan coast required no assistance from carrier aircraft.   As the CVEs of 21st ACS were reinforced by the arrival of the five carriers mentioned above, their squadrons were attached to FEAF, to gain experience in the unaccustomed techniques required for fighting and flying over the jungle.

To provide photographic coverage of the next intended operational areas, from Rangoon to the Thai/Malay border, the photo-recce Hellcats of 888 Squadron, the only specialized reconnaissance unit to operate with the Fleet Air Arm, embarked in EMPRESS.   With AMEER providing Combat Air Patrol and escort, extensive coverage of the Kra Isthmus, Penang and northern Sumatra areas was obtained between 26th February and 4th March; in addition to the good Photographic Reconnaissance results, the Hellcats obtained their first victories off Burma when 804 Squadron destroyed three Japanese aircraft on 1st March. EMPEROR and KHEDIVE undertook their first operation in April, combining PR with strikes on Sumatran targets between 12th and 16th, damaging a 4,000grt freighter off Emmahaven and destroying at least three more enemy aircraft (808).

These small-scale operations provided experience for the CVEs and aircrew, which was put to effect in the amphibious operation to occupy Rangoon.   Operation "Dracula" was robbed of much of its effect by the fact that the landings were unopposed, so that there was little trade for the 100-odd Hellcats and Seafires embarked in EMPEROR, KHEDIVE, HUNTER and STALKER.   The carriers met the main invasion convoy off Akyab on 30th April and flew 72 protective sorties on that day and the next, following this up with 110 on D-Day, 2nd May, the majority being fighter-bomber missions over the beaches and the town.   Bad weather followed on 3rd and 4th, and at the end of this period the carrier group moved south to strike at enemy airfields and shipping off the Tenasserim coast, on 5th and 6th May.

Meanwhile SHAH and EMPRESS had sailed with the main strength of the 3rd Battle Squadron to cover against interference from Japanese units based on Singapore and to neutralise enemy airfields in the Andamans and Nicobar Islands.   The carrier aircraft struck with rockets and bombs and spotted for bombardment by the capital ships.   The archipelagoes were attacked on 30th April and 1st and 2nd May, before the force turned its attention to Japanese positions around Tavoy, on the Burmese coast where considerable damage was caused up to the 7th May, when the 3rd BS withdrew, returning to Trincomalee in the afternoon of 9th, a few hours after the four CVEs of 21st Aircraft Carrier Squadron.   The six small carriers had flown over 400 sorties in eight days, for the loss of just two Hellcats to enemy action.   There were 19 Seafire deck-landing accidents, six of them resulting in write-offs; again the light winds and small carriers had proved inadequate for the Seafire.

Shortly after the return of the CVE groups, intelligence was received of an impending enemy reinforcement of the Andamans and the main strength of the 3rd BS sailed within 24 hours of their return to Trincomalee. SHAH, EMPEROR, EMPRESS and KHEDIVE accompanied the force, with 62 Hellcats and nine Avengers between them. A sighting report was received from patrolling submarines in the Malacca Straits stating that the cruiser HAGURO and three smaller warships had been sighted heading north-west. On 11th May, advantage was taken of the proximity of the CVE force to Car Nicobar to launch a Hellcat strike which destroyed a few more Japanese aircraft on the airfield. The strike probably alerted the enemy to the presence of a powerful naval force awaiting HAGURO and her consorts. The cruiser turned back, but the Andamans garrison was in dire straits, and she had to make a further attempt on 15th May. As one of the submarines had sighted HAGURO heading back for Singapore, the CVEs were directed to locate and attack enemy merchant shipping in the Malacca Straits. Unfortunately SHAH's catapult became unserviceable and her Avengers had to be transferred to EMPEROR, an Assault CVE without the facilities for arming and briefing a Torpedo Bomber Reconnaissance strike. One of the Avengers found the cruiser and a destroyer off Sabang, just before noon on 15th, while the aircraft was searching for the merchantmen.

Due to the congestion on EMPEROR's deck, insufficient Avengers were available for shadowing and only three could be launched, an hour and a half later, to strike at the cruiser. The aircraft regained contact with the enemy after two hours and the dive-bombing resulted in just one very near-miss forward. Little more could be expected with such a small force with scant recent training in the shipping strike role and operating under such adverse conditions. It fell to the 26th Destroyer Flotilla, detached from the main body to deal with the merchant ships, to find and destroy HAGURO in a well-executed night torpedo attack (in the best traditions of the Imperial Japanese Navy), in the early hours of 16th May.

After the failure on the part of the enemy to supply their garrison in the Andamans, HUNTER and KHEDIVE were despatched to strike at the remains of the small warships and shipping in the Islands, and to spread general "alarm and despondency". Throughout June 1945 the CVEs kept up the pressure against enemy shipping off the coasts of Sumatra and the sub-continent. Heavy air strikes were delivered against the Sabang and Medan airfields, destroying more than half of the enemy aircraft remaining on Sumatra. Vast damage was inflicted on railway stock in Sumatra and in southern Burma, while 888 took more photographs, of the Penang area on this occasion.

In mid-July EMPEROR, STALKER and AMEER destroyed the last of the enemy aircraft on Car Nicobar, flown in since the last operation, together with the last of the small craft used to supply the outlying islands of the group. The last operation executed by the CVEs was the protection of minesweeping forces off Phuket Island, South Thailand. AMEER and EMPRESS did not restrict their flying to Combat Air

Patrol, but their Hellcats carried out far-ranging attacks on enemy airfields at Sungei Patani, Bandan and Alor Star. In three days of operations, from 24th to 26th July, the carriers flew over 150 Hellcat sorties to destroy more than 30 enemy aircraft on the ground, about an equal number of railway locomotives, and countless targets among the enemy motor transport. On 26th July the force was attacked by the only Kamikazes to be met in the Bay of Bengal. Only about seven enemy aircraft were involved, and the CAP shot down three before the raid reached the Gun Defence Zone. Of the two which found targets, one sank the 'sweeper VESTAL, while the other hit and set afire AMEER. The fire was soon extinguished and the ship was able to return to Akyab under her own steam, and was even ready to participate in the next sortie by 21st ACS. This last operation was a planned strike on Penang, cancelled on 11th August 1945, and included ATTACKER, EMPEROR, HUNTER and SHAH, in addition to AMEER. These ships, joined by BEGUM and STALKER, subsequently covered the re-occupation of Malaya and Singapore in late August and September.

By VJ-Day there were nine Assault CVEs and four Strike CVEs, with 220 fighters and 40 strike aircraft based on Trincomalee and Akyab, five of which had joined the Fleet too late to see action, but all of which had seen action at some time or other, from Bodo to Burma. In addition there were reserve front-line squadrons ashore working up for embarked operations.

It was estimated that the aircraft of 21st Aircraft Carrier Squadron destroyed more than a third of the serviceable Japanese aircraft in Burma, Malaya and Sumatra in the course of the last six months of the War, together with a vast amount of coastal shipping, railway stock and motor transport. Japanese records are so contradictory that it is difficult to assess exactly what their losses were, but there is no doubt that the aircraft, and the destroyers, for which the Hellcats provided Combat Air Patrols during sweeps, effectively strangled enemy movements by sea in the last few months. Losses to the carrier aircraft from enemy action were insignificant, more being written off in landing accidents associated with the light wind conditions prevailing for most of the operations. Unlike the carrier support afforded off Okinawa, the East Indies Fleet CVE operations were an extension of land-based air power, rather than the substitute provided by the Fleet carriers, and their rather than the substitute provided by the Fleet carriers, and their activities were somewhat circumscribed for long-range operations by the lack of a Fleet Train, the British Pacific Fleet enjoying absolute priority in this respect.

By the end of 1945, the CVEs had left the East Indies Fleet, replaced by a couple of Light Fleet Carriers, and of all the Hellcats only 888 Squadron continued, carrying out the first aerial survey of South East Asia, until August 1946, when they disbanded.

DISPOSITION OF VESSELS AND SQUADRONS

Ramree (21st and end of January) and Cheduba Is. (26th January) 1945
AMEER
804 Squadron   24 Hellcats

Photographic reconnaissance — February and March 1945
EMPRESS
888 Squadron   8 Hellcat PR IIs
804   „   4 Hellcats IIs (detachment)
845   „   8 Avengers
AMEER
804 Squadron   20 Hellcats

Photographic reconnaissance — April 1945
EMPEROR
888 Squadron   4 Hellcat PR IIs
808   „   4 Hellcat IIs
851   „   8 Avenger IIs
KHEDIVE
808 Squadron   20 Hellcats

Operation DRACULA — Rangoon — 2nd to 6th May 1945
EMPEROR
800 Squadron   24 Hellcats
1700   „   1 Sea Otter (Rescue detachment)
HUNTER
807 Squadron   29 Seafires
1700   „   1 Sea Otter
KHEDIVE
808 Squadron   24 Hellcats
STALKER
809 Squadron   30 Seafires

Diversionary strikes 30th April to 7th May 1945
EMPRESS
804 Squadron   20 Hellcats
SHAH
851 Squadron   12 Avengers
804   „   4 Hellcats
Forces for HAGURO search and strike in text

Andamans strikes — May 1945
HUNTER
807 Squadron   30 Seafires
KHEDIVE
808 Squadron   24 Hellcats
1700   „   1 Sea Otter

Burma and Sumatra strikes — June 1945
AMEER
804 Squadron   20 Hellcats
1700   „   1 Sea Otter
888   „   4 Hellcat PR IIs
EMPEROR
800 Squadron   16 Hellcats
1700   „   1 Sea Otter
KHEDIVE
808 Squadron   24 Hellcats
SHAH
800 Squadron   8 Hellcats
845   „   4 Avengers
851   „   8 Avengers
STALKER
809 Squadron   30 Seafires
1700   „   1 Sea Otter

DISPOSITION—continued

Nicobars — July 1945
EMPEROR
    800 Squadron   24 Hellcats
AMEER
    896 Squadron   24 Hellcats
STALKER
    809 Squadron   30 Seafires

Minesweeping off Phuket Is. July 1945
AMEER — damaged by Kamikaze on 26th July
    804 Squadron   24 Hellcats
    1700   ,,   1 Sea Otter
EMPRESS
    896 Squadron   24 Hellcats

Cancelled strike on Penang — August 1945
EMPEROR
    800 Squadron   24 Hellcats
HUNTER
    807 Squadron   30 Seafires
    1700   ,,   1 Sea Otter
ATTACKER
    879 Squadron   30 Seafires
SHAH
    851 Squadron   8 Avengers
    845   ,,   8 Avengers
EMPRESS
    896 Squadron   24 Hellcats
AMEER
    804 Squadron   24 Hellcats

Section 5

THE BRITISH PACIFIC FLEET

Palembang—January 1945

The main striking force of the British Pacific Fleet left Trincomalee on 16th January 1945, bound for Sydney, which was to be the main Fleet base for Pacific operations. En route the carriers undertook strikes on the Sumatran oil refineries around Palembang.

The strike on the Pladjoe refinery was postponed from 22nd to 24th January due to bad weather in the launch area, and 43 Avengers, armed with 172 500 lb bombs, supported by 12 rocket-firing Fireflies and about 50 fighters, attacked the oil installation on the latter day. In order to prevent the enemy fighters from reacting in strength, four Avengers and part of the fighter escort attacked the principal airfields in the target area. The co-ordination of the attack was highly successful, no enemy aircraft being encountered before the strike, while the flak did not open fire until the Avengers and Fireflies were in their dives. An unexpected hazard, however, was the presence of balloons, which caused the loss of no aircraft from this particular strike. The output of the refinery was halved for three months and most of the oil in the storage tanks was burnt out as a result of the attack. The fighter sweep destroyed 34 enemy aircraft on the airfields, but were unable to prevent all the Japanese fighters from getting airborne. The rendezvous and form-up area for the Avengers was in a heavily defended area, and the

---

DISPOSITION OF VESSELS AND SQUADRONS

Pladjoe and Soengi Gerong — January 1945
INDOMITABLE — Flag Rear Admiral Vian

1839 Squadron	14 Hellcats
1844 „	14 Hellcats
857 „	21 Avengers

ILLUSTRIOUS

1830 Squadron	14 Corsairs
1833 „	14 Corsairs
854 „	21 Avengers

VICTORIOUS

1834 Squadron	14 Corsairs
1836 „	14 Corsairs
849 „	21 Avengers
Ship's Flight	2 Walruses (Search and Rescue detachment)

INDEFATIGABLE

887 Squadron	20 Seafires
894 „	20 Seafires
1770 „	12 Fireflies
820 „	21 Avengers

enemy flak badly damaged several of the strike aircraft, although only two Avengers were lost, the crew of one being rescued. The escort accounted for 14 enemy aircraft, for the loss of a grand total of seven Fleet Air Arm aircraft from all causes.

The Pladjoe strike was followed, on 29th January, by an even more successful attack on the Soengi Gerong refinery, also in the Palembang vicinity. Approximately the same number of striking aircraft was involved, but a revised rendezvous position was briefed and the fighter sweep concentrated on the two major airfields. Although the Fireflies were detailed to strafe the balloons during their rocket dives, two Avengers were lost in this manner. The strike was pressed home, and such was the accuracy of the weapons delivery that all production was stopped for two months, and when deliveries were re-commenced, they were a mere fraction of the pre-strike output. In addition to 38 enemy aircraft destroyed on the ground by the fighter sweep, over 30 were shot down by the escort, but several Avengers were lost to the enemy fighters. Altogether, 16 Fleet Air Arm aircraft were lost over the target area to enemy action. Enemy reconnaissance aircraft found the Fleet, but were driven off by the Combat Air Patrol and A-A. Two G4Ms were shot down by one Hellcat pilot, who in turn was damaged by "friendly" A-A from KING GEORGE V, but managed to land back aboard INDOMITABLE. No enemy attacks materialised against the Fleet and after recovering she strike the carriers and their consorts headed for Freemantle and Sydney.

At a cost to the Royal Navy of 25 aircraft, the air groups of INDOMITABLE, ILLUSTRIOUS, VICTORIOUS and INDEFATIGABLE had cut the aviation gasoline output from Sumatra to 35% of its normal level, at a time when Japan was desperately short of oil in any form. The effects of the resulting shortage on the campaigns in Burma, the Philippines, China and Okinawa are incalculable, but it is probable that the three strikes undertaken in January 1945, against Pangkalan Brandon, Pladjoe and Soengi Gerong, were the British Pacific Fleet's greatest contributions to the ultimate victory. A few merchant ships were attacked in the course of the strikes: at Pladjoe one of Japan's largest surviving tankers was damaged beyond repair. Enemy aircraft losses to the fighter sweeps, close escort, and Fleet CAP amounted to about 140 aircraft of all types.

Okinawa: The Sakishima Gunto—March to May 1945

The main body of the British Pacific Fleet arrived in Sydney on 10th February 1945 and began to prepare for joining the American Fleet, although at that date it was uncertain as to which American Fleet was involved. General MacArthur, whose naval support forces included only CVEs, wanted the BPF for the forthcoming amphibious campaigns in Borneo and Mindanao, while Admiral Nimitz, C-in-C Pacific, regarded the armoured carriers as his "most flexible reserve" and wished to commit them to the support of the landings on Okinawa. It was not until the beginning of March that the Joint Chiefs of Staff decided that Nimitz had greater need of the four Fleet carriers with their 238 aircraft.

The problems confronting the Royal Navy before it could commence operations with the highly mobile Fast Carrier Striking Force were considerable. The matter of adopting US Navy standard operating procedures in the form of signals, tactical doctrine and carrier operating technique was straightforward, if hard work for the departments concerned. The major impediment both at the outset and to the end of Pacific operations, was the lack of a properly equipped underway replenishment force. The Fleet Train, consisting of oilers, supply and stores ships, repair ships, and the special support ships required to maintain an aircraft carrier squadron at sea for weeks, never reached the strength envisaged by the Admiralty. Those that there were flew not only the White, Blue and Red Ensigns but also the merchant ensigns of many Allied nations, so hard-pressed was the Ministry of War Transport after five and a half years of a war in which some of the heaviest losses had been among vessels of the types most needed by the Fleet Train. The needs of the carriers were largely met by CVEs employed as ferry carriers, repair ships and stores carriers, as well as the few auxiliaries fitted out for these tasks.

When the British Pacific Fleet arrived at Manus, in the Admiralty Islands, at the end of February 1945, there were only 27 out of the 69 ships constituting the Fleet Train awaiting the warships in the anchorage; the remainder had been delayed by Communist-inspired strikes in the Sydney docks. After the decision to incorporate the BPF as Task Force 57 in Admiral Spruance's 5th Fleet, the Fleet replenished and left for Ulithi atoll in the Caroline Islands, arriving on 19th March 1945.

Meanwhile, Task Force 58, the USN Fast Carrier Striking Forces, had been striking at the Bonin Islands, in support of the Iwo Jima landings, at Kyushu, and at Okinawa. The intention was to destroy as many Japanese aircraft as possible prior to the landings on Okinawa; a vast number of enemy aircraft was destroyed, both on their airfields and in air combat, but on 19th March three Attack carriers, corresponding to the Royal Navy's Fleet carriers, were badly damaged off Kyushu. INTREPID and WASP were sufficiently damaged to prevent their participation in the early stages of Operation "Iceberg"—Okinawa, while FRANKLIN lost over 700 men killed by bombs and the ensuing fires and was too badly damaged to see further service in the Second World War.

The BPF—INDEFATIGABLE, INDOMITABLE, VICTORIOUS and ILLUSTRIOUS, supported by KING GEORGE V, HOWE, SWIFTSURE, GAMBIA, BLACK PRINCE, EURYALUS, ARGONAUT and 11 destroyers, left Ulithi on 23rd March with orders to keep enemy airfields in the Sakishima Gunto group of islands out of action while the Americans secured first the Kerama Retto, some 15 miles from Okinawa, and then Okinawa itself. Sakishima Gunto lies to the south west of the main Ryukyu group, and on the islands of Miyako, Ishigaki and Mihara there were six airfields which were in a favourable position to act as staging posts for aircraft based in Formosa to pass through en route for Okinawa, as well as ideally situated for a positive contribution to the defence of the main target area for "Iceberg". The British Pacific Fleet was planned to mount the heaviest possible strikes against the airfields, concentrating on the cratering of the runways, to render them useless. Operations were planned for two-day strike serials alternating with two-day replenishment serials; while the BPF were off-station, the USN CVEs SANTEE, SUWANEE, CHENANGO and STEAMER BAY, Task Group 52.1.3, took over. With their smaller aircraft complements the CVEs were not so efficient in the suppression role, a fact which became evident as the Japanese counter-attacked in mid-April.

On 26th March 1945, the first strikes were launched from a position some 100 miles to the south of the Sakishima Gunto, attacking the airfields on the two main islands. Avengers were armed with 4×500 lb medium capacity bombs for the task of breaking up the runways and destroying "hard" installations, such as hangars, buildings and fuel dumps, while INDEFATIGABLE's Fireflies used cannon and rockets against the heavy flak emplacements. Corsairs and Hellcats provided escort and target CAP, strafing targets of opportunity during and after the strikes. Fleet Combat Air Patrol was provided mainly by the Sea-fires, whose limited endurance detracted from their value as strike escort aircraft. Avenger strikes were flown, on average four times daily, with up to 40 aircraft involved in each. Some squadrons flew sorties by single Avengers, striking at targets of opportunity on the islands and achieving a certain amount of surprise. Additional Corsair and Hellcat dive-bombing sorties were flown, so that the enemy got little respite from dawn to dusk.

Despite the effort, the airfields were unrewarding targets; the runways were constructed out of crushed coral, of which there was an unlimited supply, and they were easily repaired overnight. The flak, of all calibres, was intense and very accurate, while there were few aircraft on the airfields, but more in the air, either leaving Okinawa or flying in from Formosa. The result was that after the first serial of two days only about a dozen enemy aircraft had been destroyed on the ground, while the target CAP had shot down 28 Japanese aircraft. 19 Fleet Air Arm were lost to enemy action, principally flak, in this period.

Losses were made good by the replenishment CVEs during the re-fuelling days, the latter giving the aircrew some rest before the next serial. Aircrew losses were lighter than might be expected, thanks to an excellent rescue service provided by USN "Lifeguard" submarines, destroyers from the Fleet screen and the two Walrus amphibians em-barked in VICTORIOUS for this purpose. Fighter cover for the Fleet Train came from the Hellcats of the Assault CVE SPEAKER, but during replenishment periods the Fleet carriers provided Avenger A/S patrols, maintaining four fighters at readiness on deck to back up the CAP from the escort carrier.

A typhoon warning resulted in the BPF spending three days over their first RAS (Replenishment At Sea). On 31st March, D-1 for the invasion of Okinawa, the Fleet carriers were back on station and the same round of strikes at the Sakishima airfields was recommenced. On 1st April, D-Day, the Japanese began to react strongly, combining conventional bombing with the first Kamikaze attacks encountered by the BPF. One suicide aircraft broke through the CAP and hit INDEFATIGABLE at the base of the island; instead of reducing her flight and hangar decks to a blazing shambles, the attack resulted in a short inconvenience while the debris was cleared from the armoured deck, the ship being operational within an hour of the attack. Fleet Air Arm strikes continued on 2nd April, the Fleet withdrawing that evening to replenish. Despite several attacks on the BPF, the only casualty was the destroyer ULSTER, which had to be towed to Leyte after incurring Kamikaze damage.

A further three-day serial of operations followed, from 5th to 7th April. On 6th, Kamikazes again attacked, but the only damage inflicted was by a glancing blow on ILLUSTRIOUS' island, causing no loss in the carrier's efficiency. While the BPF were refuelling on 8th April, the USN Attack carrier HANCOCK was put out of action by a Kamikaze and as it was believed that many of the Kamikaze aircraft were based in N. Formosa, Admiral Spruance requested that Task Force 57 should strike at their bases. The BPF, scheduled for only one more serial off Sakishima, willingly accepted the assignment, which was less hazardous for the armoured Fleet carriers than it would have been for the wooden-decked American carriers.

The carriers were in the launching position at dawn on 11th April, but bad weather caused a delay of 24 hours, and even when the strikes, totalling 48 Avengers supported by 40 Corsairs, did get airborne there was still a considerable amount of low cloud over the airfield targets. A few Corsairs did manage to find and attack the airfields, while the Avengers bombed the port of Kiirun, inflicting severe damage on the docks, shipping, and a chemical plant. Later in the day the Avengers did manage to find an airfield, cratering the runways while the fighters strafed aircraft on the ground and airfield installations. The strikes met with no enemy air opposition on 12th, but two Fireflies found a formation of five Japanese bombers heading towards Okinawa and shot down four, the fifth escaping damaged. That evening an enemy attack was detected heading for the Fleet; an efficient Hellcat and Corsair CAP shot down four, damaged half a dozen, and drove off the remainder before they could reach the ships.

The strikes continued in improved weather conditions on 13th April and although the enemy did intercept the Avengers, none was lost, while the escorts destroyed eight more Japanese fighters.

On completion of these operations, TF 57 withdrew to replenish prior to proceeding to San Pedro Bay, Leyte, for a week's rest and recuperation. Again their assistance was requested by Admiral Spruance; the USN CVEs had been unable to maintain in the same pressure against the airfields in the Sakishima Gunto, and there had been increased enemy air activity in the area. While the Royal Navy had been operating against the Formosan airfields, which were not as active as had been thought, the USN had been suffering heavily from the Kamikazes. Two carriers had been put out of action, three battleships were damaged, seven destroyers sunk, and another 13 damaged; enemy losses were high, but at this stage the Japanese showed no sign of easing the considerable pressure.

FORMIDABLE replaced ILLUSTRIOUS in the 1st Aircraft Carrier Squadron, the latter beginning to show signs of wear: she had not had a full refit for nearly two years, her centre shaft was giving trouble and causing a reduction in speed to 26 knots, and her No. 15 Fighter Wing, 1830 and 1833 Squadrons had done rather more than a full tour of operations. FORMIDABLE's arrival had been delayed by shaft trouble, both ships still suffering the after-effects of bomb damage received in the Mediterranean in 1941.

Strikes against Ishigakijima and Miyakojima were flown on 16th, 17th and 20th April. Another 50,000 lb of bombs were unloaded on the airfields during the three days, while enemy landing craft also suffered from the Avengers' strikes. At dusk on 20th the BPF and Fleet Train left their operational area for Leyte, the tankers almost dry and the ammunition and stores ships empty. San Pedro Bay was reached on 23rd April, the Fleet having spent 32 days at sea on operations and RAS. During the week that followed the ships were stored and replacement aircraft and aircrew transferred to the carriers. These last ships were particularly in need of rest. Fully extended at all times to keep up with the American standards of operating, the carriers were hampered by lack of handling crews, maintenance personnel and armourers: the entire ships' companies were exhausted. The climate in the Philippines was humid and the ships not air-conditioned, so that the return to sea on 1st May was welcomed by many.

While the Fleet had been at its anchorage in San Pedro Bay there had been renewed pressure for its employment off Borneo, but in view of further USN losses off Okinawa Admiral Nimitz was again allocated the BPF for covering operations off Sakishima. The air strikes were resumed on 4th May, against Ishigaki. Miyako was subjected to a bombardment by KING GEORGE V and HOWE, in the course of which much damage was inflicted by the 14 in guns. The absence of the large calibre A-A and considerable volume of close-range A-A was inopportune however; the return of TF 57 coincided with a renewed Kamikaze offensive, and during the forenoon of 4th May a force of about 20 suicide aircraft attacked the Fleet. Eight were shot down, one by the A-A after it had penetrated the screen, the others by the CAP, and of the remainder only two reached the carriers. The first hit INDOMITABLE aft on the flight deck, slid diagonally across the deck and went over the side; the other hit FORMIDABLE fair and square abeam the island, the favoured aiming point for the Kamikazes. The damage was not serious, fires were soon extinguished, and although a splinter put the centre boiler-room out of action temporarily, the ship's speed did not fall below 18 knots. The damage had been inflicted at the join of four armour plates, but the two-foot dent was swiftly patched with quick-drying cement and she was operational before dusk. As strikes

Albacores of 820 Squadron reform after a simulated torpedo strike on the Eastern Fleet (FORMIDABLE and WARSPITE)   [*IWM*

"G" of 888 Squadron in the slot—starboard beam of the carrier on joining the landing circuit—with WARSPITE in the background   [*IWM*

Martlets of 881 and 882 Squadrons aboard ILLUSTRIOUS during the Diego Suarez operation. Three Swordfish and a solitary Fulmar are parked ahead of the Martlets; the latter was intended for night fighter operations, to give the Fleet a small degree of cover in darkness   [*IWM*

ILLUSTRIOUS in the Indian Ocean.   The electric lamps and reflectors were used in place of the normal fabric "bats" to overcome glare   [*IWM*

VICTORIOUS passes through the Panama Canal with little room to spare, on her way to work up at Pearl Harbour
[IWM

VICTORIOUS with the US Pacific Fleet in the summer of 1943, preparing to fuel from a USN oiler. The Avengers and Martlets sport the USN stars, and a variety of camouflage schemes is apparent
[IWM

One of 882's Martlet IV's in VICTORIOUS' barrier   [*via J. D. Brown*

BATTLER working up prior to deployment with the Eastern Fleet. Although the CVEs never
undertook a torpedo strike operationally, the drills had to be exercised, and this Swordfish II
of 835 Squadron is being ranged with an 18″ torpedo   [*IWM*

An Avenger II of 845 Squadron lands after the strike on Soerabaya: 17th May 1944

[IWM

A Corsair II of 1830 Squadron gets the "cut" as it crosses ILLUSTRIOUS round-down. The continuous-turn approach was necessitated by the poor forward view enjoyed by the pilot, who did not roll the wings level until just before touch-down   [IWM

25th July 1944: A Corsair of 1837 Squadron takes off for a sortie over Sabang. The vortices
are a common phenomenon in humid atmospheres   [IWM

6C (JT324) of 1830 returns from the Pangkalan Brandon strike with flak damage to the starboard tailplane
[*IWM*

Barracuda 4P of 815 Squadron in collision with Hellcat 6-K of 1844 Squadron: INDOMITABLE, October 1944
[*MoD (Admiralty)*]

INDOMITABLE's 857 Squadron (Avengers) enter their dive on the Pangkalan Brandon refinery:
4th January 1945   [MoD (Admiralty)]

INDEFATIGABLE in transit through the Suez Canal in November 1944, en route for the
Eastern Fleet   [IWM

INDEFATIGABLE off Sumatra, 24th January 1945, seen from ILLUSTRIOUS   [IWM

One of 1770 Squadron's Fireflies takes off with a full load of eight 60lb rocket projectiles for the strike on the Soengi Gerong refinery, 29th January 1945   [IWM

AMEER off Ramree Island, January 1945. The Hellcat IIs are of 804 Squadron, the aircraft
in the foreground being JV316   [MoD (Admiralty)]

808 Squadron Hellcats being ranged aboard KHEDIVE during operations off Sumatra in April
1945   [IWM]

Briefing for the invasion of Rangoon aboard EMPRESS, with SHAH in the background. These two CVEs were employed as part of the covering force which operated off the Nicobar and Andamans Islands in a diversionary role, and to counter any northward movement by the Japanese from Singapore
[MoD (Admiralty)]

A Japanese freighter burns off Emmahaven after a strike by Hellcats from KHEDIVE and EMPEROR: 16th April 1945
Lt Cdr P. J. Spelling

"Black Flight" of 804 Squadron beating up EMPRESS   [*MoD* (*Admiralty*)]

Hellcat II JX788 of 896 Squadron, armed with rocket projectiles, runs up on the catapult during
EMPRESS' operations off Phuket Island at the end of July 1945   [*MoD* (*Admiralty*)]

Operating in light winds, deck-landing accidents were inevitable: three Hellcats were written off and one damaged in this accident aboard EMPRESS. Note the different colour schemes and pattern of roundels on the centre and right-hand aircraft   [MoD (Admiralty)]

K-6K of 804 Squadron flies over the fires on Medan airfield left after attacks by Hellcats and Seafires from STALKER   [MoD (Admiralty)]

STALKER and ATTACKER enter Singapore in early September 1945, during the re-occupation of the island   [*MoD (Admiralty*)]

PURSUER had arrived in the E. Indies before the termination of hostilities, and her 898 Squadron (Hellcat II) saw no combat in this theatre   [*Lt Cdr P. J. Spelling*]

Like PURSUER, SEARCHER, with her two dozen Wildcat VIs, arrived too late for operations in the E. Indies.   Sub Lieut. D. J. Frearson, the batsman, narrowly escapes injury as B-1C of 882 Squadron is damaged in a heavy landing   [*D. J. Frearson*

Mihara, one of the airfields on Miyakojima, under attack from Avengers and Fireflies of the British Pacific Fleet   [*MoD (Admiralty)*

FORMIDABLE shortly after being hit by Kamikaze on 4th May 1945 [*MoD (Admiralty)*]

main Fleet base in Ceylon, on 2nd April after exercising en route. The succeeding fortnight was spent in careful planning and rehearsal for a strike on Sabang, a harbour at the northern extremity of Sumatra.

The 27 warships of six Allied Navies sailed from Trincomalee on 16th April 1944 and after refuelling arrived at the launch position, some 100 miles south-west of Sabang Island, in the early hours of 19th. ILLUSTRIOUS launched 17 Barracudas and 13 Corsairs, while the larger SARATOGA provided 11 Avengers, 18 Dauntlesses and 24 Hellcats. The aircraft delivered a highly co-ordinated strike which was opposed only by flak, the latter only opening fire after the attack was well under way. There was little shipping present in the harbour, but one small freighter was sunk and another damaged and driven aground; oil storage tanks were destroyed and heavy damage inflicted upon the port facilities. In a suppressive sweep over the airfields, the Corsair and Hellcats destroyed 24 enemy aircraft on the ground. Only one aircraft, a Hellcat, was lost from the strike, and the pilot was rescued by an RN submarine stationed off the coast for that purpose. Not until the Fleet withdrew did the Japanese attempt to attack the Fleet, but the three G4M torpedo bombers were quickly "splashed" by Hellcats of the Combat Air Patrol.

On return to Trinco SARATOGA was ordered to return to the United States for a refit and it was decided to combine her eastward passage with a strike on the important aviation fuel store at Soerabaya (Surabaja) in Java. As the target was closer to Western Australia than to Ceylon the Fleet staged through Exmouth Gulf to re-fuel before arriving at the flying-off position some 180 miles south of Soerabaya just after daybreak on 17th May 1944. ILLUSTRIOUS' Barracudas had given way to Avengers as the distance to the target (across the breadth of Java) was too great for the Barra. The strike consisted of 45 Avengers and Dauntlesses, escorted by 40 Corsairs and Hellcats, attacking in two waves. One struck at the refinery while the other went for the dockyard and shipping in the harbour. Surprise was again achieved, but the results were slender. One small ship (1,000 grt) was sunk and little damage was done to the refinery. Fortunately only one aircraft was lost.

The lack of success enjoyed by the strikes became evident at the debriefing, but, following the then-current Royal Navy practice, the C-in-C was aboard a capital ship rather than a carrier, and it was not until the carriers had withdrawn far enough for a restrike to be impracticable that Somerville learnt of the disappointing results. The Fleet split up shortly after the withdrawal began, SARATOGA and her three destroyers returning to Pearl Harbour while the other ships returned to Trincomalee.

ILLUSTRIOUS' next operation was a raid on the Andaman Islands on 22nd June 1944. It was her first and only solo operation in this phase, and owing to bad weather in the target area the Barracudas had little success against the few targets available. Several Japanese aircraft were destroyed by strafing on the airfield at Port Blair, and a few small coastal vessels were sunk by the dive-bombers. Lack of adequate intelligence robbed many of the strikes of this period of the force which they might otherwise have had, while overt reconnaissance would have alerted the enemy to the likelihood of imminent carrier strikes.

In early July, the Eastern Fleet was reinforced by the arrival of VICTORIOUS, fresh from her Norwegian strikes, and INDOMITABLE, recently returned to service after the torpedo damage incurred off Sicily a year before. VICTORIOUS joined ILLUSTRIOUS in what proved to be Admiral Somerville's last operation prior to relief by Admiral Sir Bruce Fraser. This operation was a bombardment of Sabang, the target of the April strike. To provide full defensive cover for the attack ILLUSTRIOUS landed most of her Barracudas and replaced them with an additional fighter squadron, giving her 42 Corsairs, while VIC embarked her normal complement of 28 Corsairs and 21 Barracudas.

In addition to bombardment spotting, provided by the Corsairs, the carrier aircraft struck at shipping in the harbour, shore installations and airfields. The bombardment by three battleships, seven cruisers and two destroyers was extremely effective, while the air strikes again destroyed the oil storage tanks burnt out during the previous strike, but which had since been repaired. Again there was little shipping in the harbour, and only two small ships, totalling 1,500 tons, were sunk. Only superficial damage was inflicted on the bombarding ships, and no aircraft were lost, while the Fleet CAP shot down four enemy aircraft and sweeps over the airfields accounted for another two.

After the Sabang bombardment ILLUSTRIOUS proceeded to South Africa for a short refit, her first for over a year, and Rear Admiral C. Moody, Rear Admiral, Aircraft Carrier Squadron, took INDOMITABLE and VICTORIOUS to strike at Sumatran targets, the cement works at Indaroeng and the harbour at Emmahaven. The Barracuda attack on the cement works, the largest in South East Asia, was successful, reducing the output for several months; the strike on the port and shipping was less successful, only two ships, totalling 6,000 tons, were damaged. No enemy air opposition was encountered, and the Fleet Air Arm's losses were negligible. This operation, at the end of August 1944, was followed up with a strike, by the same ships, on the important rail centre of Sigli in northern Sumatra on 18th September. Although a fair amount of damage was done, neither Rear Admiral Moody nor Admiral Fraser were impressed with the performance of their offensive force, and an extensive training programme was initiated to raise the standard of weaponry in the strike squadrons. To be fair to the aircrew, they had suffered from lack of up-to-date knowledge of the target areas, which were at the extreme limit of the coverage of the limited long-range reconnaissance aircraft available in India at the time.

The next offensive operation by the carrier squadron was in the nature of diversionary support for the American forces about to commence the landings in Leyte Gulf. In an attempt to draw off Japanese naval forces, INDOMITABLE and VICTORIOUS struck at the Nicobar Islands for the three days preceding the assault on Leyte, simulating a pre-invasion bombardment. The enemy was fully pre-occupied with the impending events in the Phillippines, some 2,000 miles to the east, and there was no obvious reaction to the diversion. The targets were again few and far between, although there were enemy fighters encountered for the first time since the bombardment of Sabang. Half a dozen Ki 43 fighters were shot down by the Hellcats and Corsairs, at no loss to the Fleet Air Arm aircraft, giving the former type their first victories in the East Indies. The Barracudas sank a considerable number of small craft and coasters, for the loss of only one aircraft to ground-fire. The strikes, which went on for three days, from 17th to 19th October 1944, were the first in which the Allied force had remained in the combat area for more than a matter of hours. The immunity enjoyed by the Fleet, coupled with the loss of only two aircraft in three days (the other loss was on take-off) gave immeasurable confidence as to the possibilities of the carrier strike force to the personnel concerned. Underway replenishment was practiced by all the ships, as a vital preparation for the forthcoming operations in Pacific waters.

Nearly two months elapsed before the Carrier Squadron undertook another operation. The intervening time was taken up with intensive weapons training and working up with the Avengers which replaced the Barracudas after the Nicobars operation. ILLUSTRIOUS rejoined the Fleet, and INDEFATIGABLE joined from the Home Fleet, embarking between them some 120 Corsairs, Avengers, Seafires and Fireflies.

To a formidable carrier force was added a formidable commander in the person of Sir Philip Vian, who had commanded the escort carriers off Salerno, after a brilliant career in destroyers and cruisers.

Unfortunately the first operation under Rear Admiral Vian proved abortive due to bad weather; a strike force of 27 Avengers and 28 Corsairs and Hellcats which had set out for the refinery at Pangkalan Brandon in Sumatra, on 20th December 1944, being forced to strike at the secondary target instead. The latter, the port of Belawan Deli, near Medan, was obscured by low cloud and heavy squalls, and the strike achieved only modest results. No aircraft were lost, and as the Fleet withdrew, fighters attacked the airfields in the vicinity of Sabang, destroying several Japanese aircraft on the ground.

After returning to Trincomalee, Vian stayed long enough to add INDEFAT. to his strength before sortie-ing once again for a re-strike on Pangkalan Brandon. The combined Air Groups attacked on 4th January 1945, Avengers and Fireflies bombing and rocketing, while Corsairs and Hellcats carried out a sweep over enemy airfields before the strike, as well as providing close escort for the strike aircraft. The strike, executed in good weather, was a complete success. Heavy damage was inflicted on the refinery, considerably reducing the output, while the fighters destroyed about a dozen enemy aircraft in air combat, and another 20 of all types in strafing attacks on the airfields. The cost to the strike was one Avenger, the crew being rescued. This operation was conducted by the last Fleet carrier force to sortie from and return to Trincomalee—Scapa Flow in Technicolor, as it was known to the thousands of men with the Eastern Fleet.

By the end of 1944 agreement had at last been reached as to the conditions of employment for the British Pacific Fleet in what had been hitherto an exclusively American operational area. Accordingly, the

DISPOSITION OF VESSELS AND SQUADRONS

Sabang (April) and Soerabaya (May) 1944
ILLUSTRIOUS (Barracudas for Sabang, Avengers for Soerabaya, strikes)
1830 Squadron	14 Corsairs	
1833 ,,	14 Corsairs	
810 ,,	12 Barracudas—replaced by 832 Squadron—12 Avengers
847 ,,	9 Barracudas—replaced by 845 Squadron—12 Avengers

SARATOGA
VF 12	26 F6F-3 Hellcats
VB 12	24 SBD-5 Dauntlesses
VT 12	18 TBF-1 Avengers
Air Group Leader	1 F6F-3

Andamans Strike — 22nd June 1944
ILLUSTRIOUS — complement as Sabang strike

Bombardment of Sabang — 25th July 1944
ILLUSTRIOUS
1830 Squadron	14 Corsairs
1833 ,,	14 Corsairs
1837 ,,	14 Corsairs

VICTORIOUS
1834 Squadron	14 Corsairs
1836 ,,	14 Corsairs
831 ,,	21 Barracudas

Emmahaven and Indaroeng Strike — 29th August 1944
VICTORIOUS
1834 Squadron	14 Corsairs (top cover Emmahaven)
1836 ,,	14 Corsairs (top cover Indaroeng)
831 ,,	21 Barracudas (both targets)

INDOMITABLE — Flag Rear Admiral C. Moody RN
1839 Squadron	10 Hellcats
1844 ,,	10 Hellcats
815 ,,	12 Barracudas (Emmahaven)
817 ,,	12 Barracudas (Indaroeng)

Sigli Strike — 18th September 1944
VICTORIOUS
1834 Squadron	14 Corsairs
1836 ,,	14 Corsairs
822 ,,	21 Barracudas

INDOMITABLE — complement as Emmahaven/Indaroeng strike

Strikes on Nicobar Is. 17th to 19th October 1944
VICTORIOUS
1834 Squadron	14 Corsairs
1836 ,,	14 Corsairs
831 ,,	21 Barracudas

INDOMITABLE
1839 Squadron	14 Hellcats
1844 ,,	14 Hellcats
815 ,,	12 Barracudas
817 ,,	12 Barracudas

Belawan Deli — 21st December 1944
ILLUSTRIOUS
1830 Squadron	14 Corsairs
1833 ,,	14 Corsairs
854 ,,	21 Avengers

INDOMITABLE — Flag Rear Admiral Vian
1839 Squadron	14 Hellcats
1844 ,,	14 Hellcats
857 ,,	21 Avengers

DISPOSITION—continued

PANGKALAN BRANDON — re-strike 4th January 1945
INDOMITABLE — unchanged aircraft complement
VICTORIOUS

1834 Squadron	14 Corsairs
1836 „	14 Corsairs
849 „	21 Avengers

INDEFATIGABLE

888 Squadron	8 Hellcats (PR detachment)
887 „	16 Seafire 111s
894 „	16 Seafire 111s
1770 „	12 Fireflies
820 „	21 Avengers

main striking force of the Eastern Fleet was re-designated and on 16th January 1945 INDEFATIGABLE, INDOMITABLE, VICTORIOUS, ILLUSTRIOUS, KING GEORGE V, three cruisers and 10 destroyers left Ceylon for Sydney, to strike at the oil installations at Palembang en route.

The East Indies Fleet in 1945

With the departure of the British Pacific Fleet in January 1945, only three operational escort carriers were available for duties with a reduced battle-squadron, which comprised QUEEN ELIZABETH, RENOWN, and the French RICHELIEU. The only Assault CVE was AMEER, the others being EMPRESS and SHAH, both armed with Avengers and a Wildcat fighter flight; these fighter flights saw no combat in 1945, as the trade protection ships usually embarked flights or squadrons of Hellcats for specific operations. EMPEROR, HUNTER, KHEDIVE, STALKER and ATTACKER were all earmarked for the 21st Aircraft Carrier Squadron, the air component of the East Indies Fleet, but did not leave the Mediterranean until the end of 1944, becoming operational in the Bay of Bengal from the end of March 1945.

The primary role of the East Indies Fleet was the offshore support of the Fourteenth Army in Burma; a subsidiary role was to contain the single cruiser division which the Japanese maintained at Singapore. The remainder of the Imperial Japanese Navy's strength was in home waters— what was left of it after the Battles of the Philippine Sea, Surigao Strait, and Cape Engano, and the depradations of the USN submarines.

The first operation undertaken by a CVE after Vice Admiral Sir Arthur Power had taken command of the East Indies Fleet in January 1945 was in support of landings on Ramree Island, one of the operations supplementary to the assault on Akyab. AMEER's Hellcats provided Combat Air Patrol over the bombarding QUEEN ELIZABETH and PHOEBE, while the Far East Air Force gave the landing forces close support. After this operation, on 21st January, AMEER went on to supply all the air cover for a Royal Marines landing on Cheduba Island on 26th, dive-bombing and strafing enemy defensive positions. Meanwhile the Japanese defenders on Ramree were fighting stubbornly and to hasten the full occupation of the island landings were made in the south, covered by AMEER.   The Hellcats again attacked enemy positions ashore, greatly assisting the troops in their advance.

After the vital base of Akyab had been secured, XIV Army's main preoccupation was with the break-out from the Imphal Plain, well inland, and the subsequent drive on Mandalay, and such small amphibious operations as were carried out on the Arakan coast required no assistance from carrier aircraft.   As the CVEs of 21st ACS were reinforced by the arrival of the five carriers mentioned above, their squadrons were attached to FEAF, to gain experience in the unaccustomed techniques required for fighting and flying over the jungle.

To provide photographic coverage of the next intended operational areas, from Rangoon to the Thai/Malay border, the photo-recce Hellcats of 888 Squadron, the only specialized reconnaissance unit to operate with the Fleet Air Arm, embarked in EMPRESS.   With AMEER providing Combat Air Patrol and escort, extensive coverage of the Kra Isthmus, Penang and northern Sumatra areas was obtained between 26th February and 4th March; in addition to the good Photographic Reconnaissance results, the Hellcats obtained their first victories off Burma when 804 Squadron destroyed three Japanese aircraft on 1st March. EMPEROR and KHEDIVE undertook their first operation in April, combining PR with strikes on Sumatran targets between 12th and 16th, damaging a 4,000grt freighter off Emmahaven and destroying at least three more enemy aircraft (808).

These small-scale operations provided experience for the CVEs and aircrew, which was put to effect in the amphibious operation to occupy Rangoon.   Operation "Dracula" was robbed of much of its effect by the fact that the landings were unopposed, so that there was little trade for the 100-odd Hellcats and Seafires embarked in EMPEROR, KHEDIVE, HUNTER and STALKER.   The carriers met the main invasion convoy off Akyab on 30th April and flew 72 protective sorties on that day and the next, following this up with 110 on D-Day, 2nd May, the majority being fighter-bomber missions over the beaches and the town.   Bad weather followed on 3rd and 4th, and at the end of this period the carrier group moved south to strike at enemy airfields and shipping off the Tenasserim coast, on 5th and 6th May.

Meanwhile SHAH and EMPRESS had sailed with the main strength of the 3rd Battle Squadron to cover against interference from Japanese units based on Singapore and to neutralise enemy airfields in the Andamans and Nicobar Islands.   The carrier aircraft struck with rockets and bombs and spotted for bombardment by the capital ships.   The archipelagoes were attacked on 30th April and 1st and 2nd May, before the force turned its attention to Japanese positions around Tavoy, on the Burmese coast where considerable damage was caused up to the 7th May, when the 3rd BS withdrew, returning to Trincomalee in the afternoon of 9th, a few hours after the four CVEs of 21st Aircraft Carrier Squadron.   The six small carriers had flown over 400 sorties in eight days, for the loss of just two Hellcats to enemy action.   There were 19 Seafire decklanding accidents, six of them resulting in write-offs; again the light winds and small carriers had proved inadequate for the Seafire.

Shortly after the return of the CVE groups, intelligence was received of an impending enemy reinforcement of the Andamans and the main strength of the 3rd BS sailed within 24 hours of their return to Trincomalee. SHAH, EMPEROR, EMPRESS and KHEDIVE accompanied the force, with 62 Hellcats and nine Avengers between them. A sighting report was received from patrolling submarines in the Malacca Straits stating that the cruiser HAGURO and three smaller warships had been sighted heading north-west. On 11th May, advantage was taken of the proximity of the CVE force to Car Nicobar to launch a Hellcat strike which destroyed a few more Japanese aircraft on the airfield. The strike probably alerted the enemy to the presence of a powerful naval force awaiting HAGURO and her consorts. The cruiser turned back, but the Andamans garrison was in dire straits, and she had to make a further attempt on 15th May. As one of the submarines had sighted HAGURO heading back for Singapore, the CVEs were directed to locate and attack enemy merchant shipping in the Malacca Straits. Unfortunately SHAH's catapult became unserviceable and her Avengers had to be transferred to EMPEROR, an Assault CVE without the facilities for arming and briefing a Torpedo Bomber Reconnaissance strike. One of the Avengers found the cruiser and a destroyer off Sabang, just before noon on 15th, while the aircraft was searching for the merchantmen.

Due to the congestion on EMPEROR's deck, insufficient Avengers were available for shadowing and only three could be launched, an hour and a half later, to strike at the cruiser. The aircraft regained contact with the enemy after two hours and the dive-bombing resulted in just one very near-miss forward. Little more could be expected with such a small force with scant recent training in the shipping strike role and operating under such adverse conditions. It fell to the 26th Destroyer Flotilla, detached from the main body to deal with the merchant ships, to find and destroy HAGURO in a well-executed night torpedo attack (in the best traditions of the Imperial Japanese Navy), in the early hours of 16th May.

After the failure on the part of the enemy to supply their garrison in the Andamans, HUNTER and KHEDIVE were despatched to strike at the remains of the small warships and shipping in the Islands, and to spread general "alarm and despondency". Throughout June 1945 the CVEs kept up the pressure against enemy shipping off the coasts of Sumatra and the sub-continent. Heavy air strikes were delivered against the Sabang and Medan airfields, destroying more than half of the enemy aircraft remaining on Sumatra. Vast damage was inflicted on railway stock in Sumatra and in southern Burma, while 888 took more photographs, of the Penang area on this occasion.

In mid-July EMPEROR, STALKER and AMEER destroyed the last of the enemy aircraft on Car Nicobar, flown in since the last operation, together with the last of the small craft used to supply the outlying islands of the group. The last operation executed by the CVEs was the protection of minesweeping forces off Phuket Island, South Thailand. AMEER and EMPRESS did not restrict their flying to Combat Air

Patrol, but their Hellcats carried out far-ranging attacks on enemy airfields at Sungei Patani, Bandan and Alor Star. In three days of operations, from 24th to 26th July, the carriers flew over 150 Hellcat sorties to destroy more than 30 enemy aircraft on the ground, about an equal number of railway locomotives, and countless targets among the enemy motor transport. On 26th July the force was attacked by the only Kamikazes to be met in the Bay of Bengal. Only about seven enemy aircraft were involved, and the CAP shot down three before the raid reached the Gun Defence Zone. Of the two which found targets, one sank the 'sweeper VESTAL, while the other hit and set afire AMEER. The fire was soon extinguished and the ship was able to return to Akyab under her own steam, and was even ready to participate in the next sortie by 21st ACS. This last operation was a planned strike on Penang, cancelled on 11th August 1945, and included ATTACKER, EMPEROR, HUNTER and SHAH, in addition to AMEER. These ships, joined by BEGUM and STALKER, subsequently covered the re-occupation of Malaya and Singapore in late August and September.

By VJ-Day there were nine Assault CVEs and four Strike CVEs, with 220 fighters and 40 strike aircraft based on Trincomalee and Akyab, five of which had joined the Fleet too late to see action, but all of which had seen action at some time or other, from Bodo to Burma. In addition there were reserve front-line squadrons ashore working up for embarked operations.

It was estimated that the aircraft of 21st Aircraft Carrier Squadron destroyed more than a third of the serviceable Japanese aircraft in Burma, Malaya and Sumatra in the course of the last six months of the War, together with a vast amount of coastal shipping, railway stock and motor transport. Japanese records are so contradictory that it is difficult to assess exactly what their losses were, but there is no doubt that the aircraft, and the destroyers, for which the Hellcats provided Combat Air Patrols during sweeps, effectively strangled enemy movements by sea in the last few months. Losses to the carrier aircraft from enemy action were insignificant, more being written off in landing accidents associated with the light wind conditions prevailing for most of the operations. Unlike the carrier support afforded off Okinawa, the East Indies Fleet CVE operations were an extension of land-based air power, rather than the substitute provided by the Fleet carriers, and their rather than the substitute provided by the Fleet carriers, and their activities were somewhat circumscribed for long-range operations by the lack of a Fleet Train, the British Pacific Fleet enjoying absolute priority in this respect.

By the end of 1945, the CVEs had left the East Indies Fleet, replaced by a couple of Light Fleet Carriers, and of all the Hellcats only 888 Squadron continued, carrying out the first aerial survey of South East Asia, until August 1946, when they disbanded.

DISPOSITION OF VESSELS AND SQUADRONS

Ramree (21st and end of January) and Cheduba Is. (26th January) 1945
AMEER
    804 Squadron   24 Hellcats

Photographic reconnaissance — February and March 1945
EMPRESS
    888 Squadron   8 Hellcat PR IIs
    804   ,,   4 Hellcats IIs (detachment)
    845   ,,   8 Avengers
AMEER
    804 Squadron   20 Hellcats

Photographic reconnaissance — April 1945
EMPEROR
    888 Squadron   4 Hellcat PR IIs
    808   ,,   4 Hellcat IIs
    851   ,,   8 Avenger IIs
KHEDIVE
    808 Squadron   20 Hellcats

Operation DRACULA — Rangoon — 2nd to 6th May 1945
EMPEROR
    800 Squadron   24 Hellcats
    1700   ,,   1 Sea Otter (Rescue detachment)
HUNTER
    807 Squadron   29 Seafires
    1700   ,,   1 Sea Otter
KHEDIVE
    808 Squadron   24 Hellcats
STALKER
    809 Squadron   30 Seafires

Diversionary strikes 30th April to 7th May 1945
EMPRESS
    804 Squadron   20 Hellcats
SHAH
    851 Squadron   12 Avengers
    804   ,,   4 Hellcats
Forces for HAGURO search and strike in text

Andamans strikes — May 1945
HUNTER
    807 Squadron   30 Seafires
KHEDIVE
    808 Squadron   24 Hellcats
    1700   ,,   1 Sea Otter

Burma and Sumatra strikes — June 1945
AMEER
    804 Squadron   20 Hellcats
    1700   ,,   1 Sea Otter
    888   ,,   4 Hellcat PR IIs
EMPEROR
    800 Squadron   16 Hellcats
    1700   ,,   1 Sea Otter
KHEDIVE
    808 Squadron   24 Hellcats
SHAH
    800 Squadron   8 Hellcats
    845   ,,   4 Avengers
    851   ,,   8 Avengers
STALKER
    809 Squadron   30 Seafires
    1700   ,,   1 Sea Otter

DISPOSITION—continued

Nicobars — July 1945
EMPEROR
    800 Squadron   24 Hellcats
AMEER
    896 Squadron   24 Hellcats
STALKER
    809 Squadron   30 Seafires

Minesweeping off Phuket Is. July 1945
AMEER — damaged by Kamikaze on 26th July
    804 Squadron   24 Hellcats
    1700   ,,   1 Sea Otter
EMPRESS
    896 Squadron   24 Hellcats

Cancelled strike on Penang — August 1945
EMPEROR
    800 Squadron   24 Hellcats
HUNTER
    807 Squadron   30 Seafires
    1700   ,,   1 Sea Otter
ATTACKER
    879 Squadron   30 Seafires
SHAH
    851 Squadron   8 Avengers
    845   ,,   8 Avengers
EMPRESS
    896 Squadron   24 Hellcats
AMEER
    804 Squadron   24 Hellcats

Section 5

THE BRITISH PACIFIC FLEET

Palembang—January 1945

The main striking force of the British Pacific Fleet left Trincomalee on 16th January 1945, bound for Sydney, which was to be the main Fleet base for Pacific operations. En route the carriers undertook strikes on the Sumatran oil refineries around Palembang.

The strike on the Pladjoe refinery was postponed from 22nd to 24th January due to bad weather in the launch area, and 43 Avengers, armed with 172 500 lb bombs, supported by 12 rocket-firing Fireflies and about 50 fighters, attacked the oil installation on the latter day. In order to prevent the enemy fighters from reacting in strength, four Avengers and part of the fighter escort attacked the principal airfields in the target area. The co-ordination of the attack was highly successful, no enemy aircraft being encountered before the strike, while the flak did not open fire until the Avengers and Fireflies were in their dives. An unexpected hazard, however, was the presence of balloons, which caused the loss of no aircraft from this particular strike. The output of the refinery was halved for three months and most of the oil in the storage tanks was burnt out as a result of the attack. The fighter sweep destroyed 34 enemy aircraft on the airfields, but were unable to prevent all the Japanese fighters from getting airborne. The rendezvous and form-up area for the Avengers was in a heavily defended area, and the

---

DISPOSITION OF VESSELS AND SQUADRONS

Pladjoe and Soengi Gerong — January 1945

INDOMITABLE — Flag Rear Admiral Vian

1839 Squadron	14 Hellcats	
1844 ,,	14 Hellcats	
857 ,,	21 Avengers	

ILLUSTRIOUS

1830 Squadron	14 Corsairs	
1833 ,,	14 Corsairs	
854 ,,	21 Avengers	

VICTORIOUS

1834 Squadron	14 Corsairs	
1836 ,,	14 Corsairs	
849 ,,	21 Avengers	
Ship's Flight	2 Walruses (Search and Rescue detachment)	

INDEFATIGABLE

887 Squadron	20 Seafires	
894 ,,	20 Seafires	
1770 ,,	12 Fireflies	
820 ,,	21 Avengers	

enemy flak badly damaged several of the strike aircraft, although only two Avengers were lost, the crew of one being rescued. The escort accounted for 14 enemy aircraft, for the loss of a grand total of seven Fleet Air Arm aircraft from all causes.

The Pladjoe strike was followed, on 29th January, by an even more successful attack on the Soengi Gerong refinery, also in the Palembang vicinity. Approximately the same number of striking aircraft was involved, but a revised rendezvous position was briefed and the fighter sweep concentrated on the two major airfields. Although the Fireflies were detailed to strafe the balloons during their rocket dives, two Avengers were lost in this manner. The strike was pressed home, and such was the accuracy of the weapons delivery that all production was stopped for two months, and when deliveries were re-commenced, they were a mere fraction of the pre-strike output. In addition to 38 enemy aircraft destroyed on the ground by the fighter sweep, over 30 were shot down by the escort, but several Avengers were lost to the enemy fighters. Altogether, 16 Fleet Air Arm aircraft were lost over the target area to enemy action. Enemy reconnaissance aircraft found the Fleet, but were driven off by the Combat Air Patrol and A-A. Two G4Ms were shot down by one Hellcat pilot, who in turn was damaged by "friendly" A-A from KING GEORGE V, but managed to land back aboard INDOMITABLE. No enemy attacks materialised against the Fleet and after recovering she strike the carriers and their consorts headed for Freemantle and Sydney.

At a cost to the Royal Navy of 25 aircraft, the air groups of INDOM-ITABLE, ILLUSTRIOUS, VICTORIOUS and INDEFATIGABLE had cut the aviation gasoline output from Sumatra to 35% of its normal level, at a time when Japan was desperately short of oil in any form. The effects of the resulting shortage on the campaigns in Burma, the Philippines, China and Okinawa are incalculable, but it is probable that the three strikes undertaken in January 1945, against Pangkalan Brandon, Pladjoe and Soengi Gerong, were the British Pacific Fleet's greatest contributions to the ultimate victory. A few merchant ships were attacked in the course of the strikes: at Pladjoe one of Japan's largest surviving tankers was damaged beyond repair. Enemy aircraft losses to the fighter sweeps, close escort, and Fleet CAP amounted to about 140 aircraft of all types.

Okinawa: The Sakishima Gunto—March to May 1945

The main body of the British Pacific Fleet arrived in Sydney on 10th February 1945 and began to prepare for joining the American Fleet, although at that date it was uncertain as to which American Fleet was involved. General MacArthur, whose naval support forces included only CVEs, wanted the BPF for the forthcoming amphibious campaigns in Borneo and Mindanao, while Admiral Nimitz, C-in-C Pacific, re-garded the armoured carriers as his "most flexible reserve" and wished to commit them to the support of the landings on Okinawa. It was not until the beginning of March that the Joint Chiefs of Staff decided that Nimitz had greater need of the four Fleet carriers with their 238 aircraft.

The problems confronting the Royal Navy before it could commence operations with the highly mobile Fast Carrier Striking Force were considerable. The matter of adopting US Navy standard operating procedures in the form of signals, tactical doctrine and carrier operating technique was straightforward, if hard work for the departments concerned. The major impediment both at the outset and to the end of Pacific operations, was the lack of a properly equipped underway replenishment force. The Fleet Train, consisting of oilers, supply and stores ships, repair ships, and the special support ships required to maintain an aircraft carrier squadron at sea for weeks, never reached the strength envisaged by the Admiralty. Those that there were flew not only the White, Blue and Red Ensigns but also the merchant ensigns of many Allied nations, so hard-pressed was the Ministry of War Transport after five and a half years of a war in which some of the heaviest losses had been among vessels of the types most needed by the Fleet Train. The needs of the carriers were largely met by CVEs employed as ferry carriers, repair ships and stores carriers, as well as the few auxiliaries fitted out for these tasks.

When the British Pacific Fleet arrived at Manus, in the Admiralty Islands, at the end of February 1945, there were only 27 out of the 69 ships constituting the Fleet Train awaiting the warships in the anchorage; the remainder had been delayed by Communist-inspired strikes in the Sydney docks. After the decision to incorporate the BPF as Task Force 57 in Admiral Spruance's 5th Fleet, the Fleet replenished and left for Ulithi atoll in the Caroline Islands, arriving on 19th March 1945.

Meanwhile, Task Force 58, the USN Fast Carrier Striking Forces, had been striking at the Bonin Islands, in support of the Iwo Jima landings, at Kyushu, and at Okinawa. The intention was to destroy as many Japanese aircraft as possible prior to the landings on Okinawa; a vast number of enemy aircraft was destroyed, both on their airfields and in air combat, but on 19th March three Attack carriers, corresponding to the Royal Navy's Fleet carriers, were badly damaged off Kyushu. INTREPID and WASP were sufficiently damaged to prevent their participation in the early stages of Operation "Iceberg"—Okinawa, while FRANKLIN lost over 700 men killed by bombs and the ensuing fires and was too badly damaged to see further service in the Second World War.

The BPF—INDEFATIGABLE, INDOMITABLE, VICTORIOUS and ILLUSTRIOUS, supported by KING GEORGE V, HOWE, SWIFTSURE, GAMBIA, BLACK PRINCE, EURYALUS, ARGONAUT and 11 destroyers, left Ulithi on 23rd March with orders to keep enemy airfields in the Sakishima Gunto group of islands out of action while the Americans secured first the Kerama Retto, some 15 miles from Okinawa, and then Okinawa itself. Sakishima Gunto lies to the south west of the main Ryukyu group, and on the islands of Miyako, Ishigaki and Mihara there were six airfields which were in a favourable position to act as staging posts for aircraft based in Formosa to pass through en route for Okinawa, as well as ideally situated for a positive contribution to the defence of the main target area for "Iceberg". The British Pacific Fleet was planned to mount the heaviest possible strikes against the airfields, concentrating on the cratering of the runways, to render them useless. Operations were planned for two-day strike serials alternating with two-day replenishment serials; while the BPF were off-station, the USN CVEs SANTEE, SUWANEE, CHENANGO and STEAMER BAY, Task Group 52.1.3, took over. With their smaller aircraft complements the CVEs were not so efficient in the suppression role, a fact which became evident as the Japanese counter-attacked in mid-April.

On 26th March 1945, the first strikes were launched from a position some 100 miles to the south of the Sakishima Gunto, attacking the airfields on the two main islands. Avengers were armed with 4 × 500 lb medium capacity bombs for the task of breaking up the runways and destroying "hard" installations, such as hangars, buildings and fuel dumps, while INDEFATIGABLE's Fireflies used cannon and rockets against the heavy flak emplacements. Corsairs and Hellcats provided escort and target CAP, strafing targets of opportunity during and after the strikes. Fleet Combat Air Patrol was provided mainly by the Sea-fires, whose limited endurance detracted from their value as strike escort aircraft. Avenger strikes were flown, on average four times daily, with up to 40 aircraft involved in each. Some squadrons flew sorties by single Avengers, striking at targets of opportunity on the islands and achieving a certain amount of surprise. Additional Corsair and Hellcat dive-bombing sorties were flown, so that the enemy got little respite from dawn to dusk.

Despite the effort, the airfields were unrewarding targets; the runways were constructed out of crushed coral, of which there was an unlimited supply, and they were easily repaired overnight. The flak, of all calibres, was intense and very accurate, while there were few aircraft on the airfields, but more in the air, either leaving Okinawa or flying in from Formosa. The result was that after the first serial of two days only about a dozen enemy aircraft had been destroyed on the ground, while the target CAP had shot down 28 Japanese aircraft. 19 Fleet Air Arm were lost to enemy action, principally flak, in this period.

Losses were made good by the replenishment CVEs during the re-fuelling days, the latter giving the aircrew some rest before the next serial. Aircrew losses were lighter than might be expected, thanks to an excellent rescue service provided by USN "Lifeguard" submarines, destroyers from the Fleet screen and the two Walrus amphibians em-barked in VICTORIOUS for this purpose. Fighter cover for the Fleet Train came from the Hellcats of the Assault CVE SPEAKER, but during replenishment periods the Fleet carriers provided Avenger A/S patrols, maintaining four fighters at readiness on deck to back up the CAP from the escort carrier.

A typhoon warning resulted in the BPF spending three days over their first RAS (Replenishment At Sea). On 31st March, D-1 for the invasion of Okinawa, the Fleet carriers were back on station and the same round of strikes at the Sakishima airfields was recommenced. On 1st April, D-Day, the Japanese began to react strongly, combining conventional bombing with the first Kamikaze attacks encountered by the BPF. One suicide aircraft broke through the CAP and hit INDEFATIGABLE at the base of the island; instead of reducing her flight and hangar decks to a blazing shambles, the attack resulted in a short inconvenience while the debris was cleared from the armoured deck, the ship being operational within an hour of the attack. Fleet Air Arm strikes continued on 2nd April, the Fleet withdrawing that evening to replenish. Despite several attacks on the BPF, the only casualty was the destroyer ULSTER, which had to be towed to Leyte after incurring Kamikaze damage.

A further three-day serial of operations followed, from 5th to 7th April. On 6th, Kamikazes again attacked, but the only damage inflicted was by a glancing blow on ILLUSTRIOUS' island, causing no loss in the carrier's efficiency. While the BPF were refuelling on 8th April, the USN Attack carrier HANCOCK was put out of action by a Kamikaze and as it was believed that many of the Kamikaze aircraft were based in N. Formosa, Admiral Spruance requested that Task Force 57 should strike at their bases. The BPF, scheduled for only one more serial off Sakishima, willingly accepted the assignment, which was less hazardous for the armoured Fleet carriers than it would have been for the wooden-decked American carriers.

The carriers were in the launching position at dawn on 11th April, but bad weather caused a delay of 24 hours, and even when the strikes, totalling 48 Avengers supported by 40 Corsairs, did get airborne there was still a considerable amount of low cloud over the airfield targets. A few Corsairs did manage to find and attack the airfields, while the Avengers bombed the port of Kiirun, inflicting severe damage on the docks, shipping, and a chemical plant. Later in the day the Avengers did manage to find an airfield, cratering the runways while the fighters strafed aircraft on the ground and airfield installations. The strikes met with no enemy air opposition on 12th, but two Fireflies found a formation of five Japanese bombers heading towards Okinawa and shot down four, the fifth escaping damaged. That evening an enemy attack was detected heading for the Fleet; an efficient Hellcat and Corsair CAP shot down four, damaged half a dozen, and drove off the remainder before they could reach the ships.

The strikes continued in improved weather conditions on 13th April and although the enemy did intercept the Avengers, none was lost, while the escorts destroyed eight more Japanese fighters.

On completion of these operations, TF 57 withdrew to replenish prior to proceeding to San Pedro Bay, Leyte, for a week's rest and recuperation. Again their assistance was requested by Admiral Spruance; the USN CVEs had been unable to maintain in the same pressure against the airfields in the Sakishima Gunto, and there had been increased enemy air activity in the area. While the Royal Navy had been operating against the Formosan airfields, which were not as active as had been thought, the USN had been suffering heavily from the Kamikazes. Two carriers had been put out of action, three battleships were damaged, seven destroyers sunk, and another 13 damaged; enemy losses were high, but at this stage the Japanese showed no sign of easing the considerable pressure.

FORMIDABLE replaced ILLUSTRIOUS in the 1st Aircraft Carrier Squadron, the latter beginning to show signs of wear: she had not had a full refit for nearly two years, her centre shaft was giving trouble and causing a reduction in speed to 26 knots, and her No. 15 Fighter Wing, 1830 and 1833 Squadrons had done rather more than a full tour of operations. FORMIDABLE's arrival had been delayed by shaft trouble, both ships still suffering the after-effects of bomb damage received in the Mediterranean in 1941.

Strikes against Ishigakijima and Miyakojima were flown on 16th, 17th and 20th April. Another 50,000 lb of bombs were unloaded on the airfields during the three days, while enemy landing craft also suffered from the Avengers' strikes. At dusk on 20th the BPF and Fleet Train left their operational area for Leyte, the tankers almost dry and the ammunition and stores ships empty. San Pedro Bay was reached on 23rd April, the Fleet having spent 32 days at sea on operations and RAS. During the week that followed the ships were stored and replacement aircraft and aircrew transferred to the carriers. These last ships were particularly in need of rest. Fully extended at all times to keep up with the American standards of operating, the carriers were hampered by lack of handling crews, maintenance personnel and armourers: the entire ships' companies were exhausted. The climate in the Philippines was humid and the ships not air-conditioned, so that the return to sea on 1st May was welcomed by many.

While the Fleet had been at its anchorage in San Pedro Bay there had been renewed pressure for its employment off Borneo, but in view of further USN losses off Okinawa Admiral Nimitz was again allocated the BPF for covering operations off Sakishima. The air strikes were resumed on 4th May, against Ishigaki. Miyako was subjected to a bombardment by KING GEORGE V and HOWE, in the course of which much damage was inflicted by the 14 in guns. The absence of the large calibre A-A and considerable volume of close-range A-A was inopportune however; the return of TF 57 coincided with a renewed Kamikaze offensive, and during the forenoon of 4th May a force of about 20 suicide aircraft attacked the Fleet. Eight were shot down, one by the A-A after it had penetrated the screen, the others by the CAP, and of the remainder only two reached the carriers. The first hit INDOMITABLE aft on the flight deck, slid diagonally across the deck and went over the side; the other hit FORMIDABLE fair and square abeam the island, the favoured aiming point for the Kamikazes. The damage was not serious, fires were soon extinguished, and although a splinter put the centre boiler-room out of action temporarily, the ship's speed did not fall below 18 knots. The damage had been inflicted at the join of four armour plates, but the two-foot dent was swiftly patched with quick-drying cement and she was operational before dusk. As strikes

A range of the 1st Carrier Air Group's Corsairs and Avengers running up before a strike on the Sakishima Gunto (1834, 1836, and 849 Squadrons) from VICTORIOUS   *[via R. C. Jones*

Upper photograph: A Kamikaze photographed a fraction of a second before striking INDOMITABLE; the aircraft is already on fire but continues (*lower photograph*) to strike INDOMITABLE amidships. The armoured deck withstood the impact and the KK continued down the deck and over the bows before exploding in the water   *[both MoD (Admiralty)*

9th May 1945: FORMIDABLE's after deck park, 11 Corsairs and four Avengers blaze after the ship had been hit for the second time in five days by Kamikaze. INDOMITABLE is in the foreground   (MoD (Admiralty))

VICTORIOUS returns to Sydney from the Sakishima area: 2nd June 1945   [via R. C. Jones

One of IMPLACABLE's Seafire IIIs goes over the port side, narrowly missing the batsman. The aircraft has taken a wire, but the undercarriage has collapsed and the swing has taken the aircraft over the edge of the deck
[MoD (Admiralty)]

Commander C. L. G. Evans, DSO, Commander (Flying) of IMPLACABLE: note the 90gallon auxiliary fuel tanks carried by 801 and 880 Squadrons' Seafire IIIs
[MoD (Admiralty)]

HERMES between the Wars. Few later photographs of this ship exist, the majority being lost
with the ship when she was sunk off Trincomalee   [via J. D. Brown

SLINGER ferrying Corsairs out to the British Pacific Fleet in February 1945. Up to 70 aircraft,
depending upon type, could be ferried in a CVE, while only about 30 at most could be operated
efficiently by one of these ships   [IWM

EAGLE in the Indian Ocean during raider hunting operations   [*via W. T. Speary*

A Barracuda of 860 Squadron gets the cut aboard NAIRANA. Note the different patterns of
inter-wire netting on forward and after barriers   [*Lt Cdr Van der Minne*

ARGUS' hangar deck, seen from the forward lift-well.   The non-folding Sea Hurricanes take up a considerable amount of space, although one aircraft of this type is semi-dismantled.   A Seafire IB is on the port side, aft   [IWM

ILLUSTRIOUS' hangar deck contrasts strongly with the above photograph.   All the space is fully utilized, and the reason for the cropping of the wings of the Corsair in Royal Navy service is evident—little enough deck-head clearance remaining after the modification.   At least 21 Corsairs (1830 and 1833 Squadrons) and Avengers (854 Squadron) are stowed in the hangar   [IWM

GLORY, the second Light Fleet carrier to become operational with the 11th Aircraft Carrier Squadron, with the Corsairs of 1831 Squadron in the forward deck-park. The ships of this class mounted only light AA weapons, and differed from their larger counterparts in having a relatively small island
[Lt R. Priestly-Cooper

VENERABLE enters Manus, Admiralty Islands, shortly after VJ-Day, en route for the re-occupation of Hong Kong
[via J. D. Brown

Corsair IV of 1836 Squadron taxies into the forward deck-park of VICTORIOUS after a sortie over Japan
[via R. C. Jones

were airborne at the time of the attack, only 11 aircraft were lost on deck; of 18 Corsairs airborne 14 were recovered on the following morning from the other carriers. A total of 12 Japanese aircraft were shot down by the Fleet fighters on that day.

The success of the bombardment of Miyako was evident on the following day when the striking aircraft found that the flak was less intense, and again the runways were cratered by the Avengers. FORMIDABLE's losses were made good during the replenishment on 6th and 7th May, while her wounded were transferred to a hospital ship. Bad weather hampered strikes on 8th, but on 9th the weather was good enough, not only for Fleet Air Arm strikes, but also for another Kamikaze attack on TF 57. At about 1700, a small group of enemy aircraft broke through the CAP and A-A screen and again FORMIDABLE was hit. On this occasion, her strike aircraft had been recovered after the pm strikes, and 18 Avengers and Corsairs were destroyed, but, as the flight deck was not holed by this attack, she was operational again in 50 minutes, albeit with only 15 aircraft serviceable. Another Kamikaze hit VICTORIOUS near the forward lift, setting fire to the ship and damaging the lift. While firefighting was in progress a second suicide aircraft hit her, but bounced off the flight deck, destroying another four Corsairs.

These were the last Kamikaze attacks on the BPF although two more USN Attack carriers, ENTERPRISE and BUNKER HILL, were sufficiently badly damaged to prevent their further employment in the War. Seven USN Attack and Escort carriers were hit by Kamikazes between 1st April and 15th May, all being rendered unfit for further service in the Okinawa campaign. Four Royal Navy carriers were hit squarely by suicide aircraft, two on two occasions; apart from a reduction in aircraft strength the carriers were all fully operational within a matter of hours.

After RAS on 10th and 11th May, two more two-day serials were flown against the island airfields and small craft in the group. Enemy air activity had slackened off after the large scale raids of 4th to 9th May, while TF 58 was again striking at airfields in Kyushu, land-based Marine fighters having taken the main weight of air support for the American forces ashore on Okinawa. Shipping strikes around Sakishima were stepped-up, with gratifying results.

As if FORMIDABLE had not suffered sufficient punishment, while she was replenishing on 18th May an accident in the hangar resulted in the destruction by fire of 30 aircraft in the hangar, as well as damage to the ship herself. Despite the accident, she was ready for action by night-fall, although very short of aircraft. When operations were resumed on 20th May FORMIDABLE could only provide Corsairs for Fleet and target CAP. She refuelled and left on 22nd May for Manus and Sydney, to repair her damage in time for the next series of operations. The remaining three carriers carried out another serial off Sakishima before they too left the area at dusk on 25th May 1945, with Okinawa firmly in the hands of the Americans.

The British Pacific Fleet had spent 62 days at sea, with only a break of eight days for storing ships at Leyte. Sorties over the Sakishima Gunto

DISPOSITION OF VESSELS AND SQUADRONS

Task Force 57 — The British Pacific Fleet off Sakishima
ILLUSTRIOUS 26th March to 15th April 1945

1830 Squadron	18 Corsairs
1833 „	18 Corsairs
854 „	16 Avengers

FORMIDABLE 14th April to 22nd May 1945

1841 Squadron	18 Corsairs
1842 „	18 Corsairs
848 „	18 Avengers

VICTORIOUS

1834 Squadron	19 Corsairs
1836 „	18 Corsairs
849 „	14 Avengers
Ships' Flight	2 Walruses

INDOMITABLE

1839 Squadron	15 Hellcats
1844 „	14 Hellcats
857 „	16 Avengers

INDEFATIGABLE

887 Squadron	20 Seafires
894 „	20 Seafires
1770 „	12 Fireflies
820 „	21 Avengers

---

and Formosa had been flown on 23 days. Exactly 5,335 sorties had been flown from the five Fleet carriers, in the course of which nearly one thousand tons of bombs had been dropped, half a million rounds of ammunition fired and 950 rockets released. Ninety-eight enemy aircraft were destroyed in combat, and about the same number on the airfields. The Fleet Air Arm suffered quite heavy losses—26 aircraft were lost in the air, mainly to flak, 61 in accidents (deck landings, take-off, "friendly" A-A, etc), while no fewer than 73 were destroyed in the Kamikaze attacks and in FORMID's hangar fire. 41 aircrew lost their lives and 44 personnel were killed aboard the ships, mainly in the Kamikaze damage. By contrast, BUNKER HILL lost 387 dead in the Kamikaze attack on 11th May. While the armoured deck cut the number of aircraft aboard a British Fleet carrier to half that of an American carrier of similar size, its value was made apparent in dramatic fashion on 4th and 9th May 1945.

Throughout the time at sea, the principal hindrance to operations had been the inadequate Fleet Train, Task Force 112; the tankers were slow and small, and refuelling equipment obsolete. On several occasions the Fleet was ready for the next serial only because there had been cancellations or postponements due to bad weather, either in the target area or at sea. Aircraft replenishment presented a more cheerful picture with ferry CVEs providing replacements to keep the Fleet carriers complemented. However, this was possible only by virtue of the extremely hard work of the Air Stations in Australia, modifying aircraft on delivery from the United Kingdom, 12,000 miles away, and United States, 6,000 miles in the other direction. Spares remained a problem as did modification kits: the American types in Fleet Air Arm service did not have the same degree of interchangeability with their opposite numbers in the USN as might be supposed.

The British Pacific Fleet arrived at Sydney at the beginning of June 1945, to re-arm the squadrons and rest the ships' complements prior to the next round, strikes on the Japanese home islands themselves.

DISPOSITION OF VESSELS AND SQUADRONS

Task Force 112 — The British Pacific Fleet Train
SPEAKER to 10th May 1945
  1840 Squadron   24 Hellcats
RULER from 9th May 1945
  885 Squadron   24 Hellcats
Truk (IMPLACABLE) and strikes on the Japanese Home Islands — June to August 1945
IMPLACABLE — Truk — TG 111.2 — Rear Admiral E. J. P. Brind RN
  801 Squadron   24 Seafires
  880   ,,   24 Seafires
  1771   ,,   12 Fireflies
  828   ,,   21 Avengers
RULER
  885 Squadron   24 Hellcats
Task Force 37
FORMIDABLE — Flag Rear Admiral Vian to 11th August 1945
  1841 Squadron   18 Corsairs
  1842   ,,   18 Corsairs
  1844   ,,   6 Hellcats (night-fighter and PR detachment)
  848   ,,   12 Avengers
VICTORIOUS — to 11th August 1945
  1834 Squadron   18 Corsairs
  1836   ,,   18 Corsairs
  849   ,,   18 Avengers
IMPLACABLE — to 11th August
  Air Group as Truk strikes
INDEFATIGABLE — 24th July to 14th August 1945
  887 Squadron   24 Seafires
  894   ,,   24 Seafires
  1772   ,,   12 Fireflies
  820   ,,   21 Avengers
Task Force 112 — Fleet Train
RULER
  885 Squadron   18 Hellcats and 4 Avengers

Fast Carrier Operations off Japan: 17th July to 15th August 1945

The only Fleet carrier of the British Pacific Fleet to see action during June 1945 was IMPLACABLE, which had arrived early in the month from Europe, sailing for Manus almost immediately. In order to complete her air group's work-up with some operational experience she sailed from Manus on 10th June in company with the CVE RULER, which had replaced SPEAKER in the Fleet Train in May, and five cruisers to strike at Truk, in the Caroline Islands. This once-important Japanese naval stronghold had been reduced to impotence by the repeated carrier air strikes from TF 58 and by the American strategy of isolation. There were therefore few worthwhile targets for the Avengers, Fireflies and dive-bombing Seafires, but the two days of operations,

14th and 15th, June brought the ships up to a fully operational status by the standards of the remainder of the Fleet.

On return to Manus IMPLACABLE was joined by the main body of the BPF, reduced by defects and refit requirements to FORMIDABLE, VICTORIOUS and KING GEORGE V. INDEFATIGABLE was delayed at Sydney with machinery defects and although she rejoined the Fleet at Manus she was unable to sail with them for Japanese waters, rejoining after the first series of strikes. INDOMITABLE was refitting and took no further part in major operations before the end of the War, although six of her Hellcats were transferred to FORMIDABLE, providing the Fleet with its only night-fighter defence.

The BPF sailed from Manus on 9th July to join Admiral J. S. McCain's Fast Carrier Force, TF 38, off Japan. On turnover and re-designation of the US Pacific Fleet, the Fifth under Admiral Spruance to the Third under Admiral Halsey, the former told his relief that he considered the British Pacific Fleet to be sufficiently experienced to join TF 38 as an autonomous group. Accordingly, TF 37 became virtually the fourth group of TF 38, adding its 180-odd aircraft to the 1,200 embarked in 16 American carriers. After the belated arrival of INDEFATIGABLE there were 255 Fleet Air Arm aircraft aboard the carriers of 1st ACS.

Operations commenced on 17th July 1945, at the height of the typhoon season. The USN recalled their first strikes, but the Royal Navy Corsairs and Fireflies managed to find and attack airfields and railway yards on the north coast of Honshu. That night KGV joined American battleships in bombarding the Hitachi industrial complex, in the Tokyo area.

On 18th July, the USN attacked the largest Japanese naval base—Yokosuka, in what was regarded as retribution for Pearl Harbour. For political reasons the BPF was excluded from the strikes and were allocated targets to the northeast of Tokyo, the reason given by the American Command being that the Fireflies and Seafires did not have the endurance for covering their attack aircraft. As on the previous day, adverse weather prevented all but the Corsairs from reaching the briefed objectives, and this type, flying with only two fighter wings, dropped 13$\frac{1}{2}$ tons of bombs during the two days.

Replenishment was scheduled for only two days, but the recurrent typhoon warnings and heavy weather in the RAS areas delayed the beginning of the next serial until 24th July, by which time INDEFATIGABLE had rejoined the Fleet. Again the USN undertook "private" strikes, on Kure, while the Fleet Air Arm concentrated on airfields on Shikoku and struck at shipping in the Inland Sea. Light flak was intense around the airfields and losses began to mount, particularly in the Corsair squadrons. The low cloud base hampered the shipping strikes, but on 24th six Avengers, two Corsairs and two Fireflies found and struck the Japanese escort carrier KAIYO, leaving her on fire and with her back broken for American aircraft to finish off at a later date. This strike was significant in that it was the only attack on an aircraft carrier by Royal Navy aircraft. While the USN sank a Fleet carrier and three battleships at Kure on 24th, the Fleet Air Arm had to make do with plainer fare, and apart from the damage inflicted on KAIYO, they sank destroyers, small escorts and many small coasters. Altogether 416 offensive sorties were flown by the four carriers on this day, in addition to over 100 CAP details.

Bad weather again curtailed flying on the following day but again much damage was inflicted on the enemy around the Inland Sea. That evening, just after dusk, FORMIDABLE's Hellcat detachment intercepted a group of Japanese Navy torpedo bombers heading for TF 37; two Hellcats shot down three B7As and damaged a fourth, the remainder being driven off without their attempting an attack.

Two days of replenishment were followed by more shipping strikes on 28th, 29th and 30th July. On 28th, the Inland Sea was again the principal target, the important dockyard at Harima being bombed in a dawn strike by 20 Avengers. The naval base at Maizuru, on the north coast of Honshu, was attacked by Corsairs, four destroyer escorts being sunk or damaged badly during the day. A few Japanese aircraft were shot down; air combats were rare at this stage as the Japanese had done an extremely efficient job of dispersing their aircraft in an attempt to husband their resources for the inevitable amphibious landings which the Allies would attempt at a later date. Unfortunately for the enemy the dispersal was so effective that they found it almost impossible to gather sufficient fighters to meet a threat to any one target. As a result the Allied fighters were rarely called upon to protect the strike aircraft from interference, although the flak remained intense to the end.

On 30th July, the airfields in the Tokyo plain were fogbound and the strikes had to seek alternate targets, again on the coast. At the end of the day the Fleet withdrew for replenishment, but instead of just two days in the RAS area, the combined Fleet eventually spent nine days off operations. Initially the delay was occasioned by the succession of typhoons but when refuelling was complete at the end of 3rd August, further strikes were delayed until the first atomic bomb had been dropped on Hiroshima, on 6th August.

The next serial was intended to begin on 8th August, but yet again a typhoon warning postponed operations. On 9th the weather was much improved and the Fleet Air Arm enjoyed further success against shipping south of Tokyo and off northern Honshu. Corsairs alternated with Avengers in strikes which kept up continuous pressure against the enemy's dwindling Navy and merchant fleet. Small craft suffered most heavily, but in Onagawa Wan all the shipping remaining afloat was sunk by the concerted air attacks mounted by Task Forces 37 and 38. Lieutenant R. Hampton Gray, DSC, RCNVR, led a Corsair "Ramrod" (bomb-armed strike) from FORMIDABLE's 1841 Squadron to sink the escort sloop AMAKUSA; despite being hit and set on fire by the flak, Lt. Gray pressed home the attack but lost his life when his Corsair crashed near the escort. This courageous officer, who had distinguished himself in operations since the strikes on TIRPITZ a year before, was awarded a posthumous Victoria Cross, only the second to be awarded to a naval aviator in World War II.

DISPOSITION OF VESSELS AND SQUADRONS

Task Force 38 — The United States Navy Task Carrier Striking Force 10th July 1945 to 14th August 1945 (Air Groups given where known)

SHANGRI LA	Flagship Vice Admiral J. S. McCain USN
BENNINGTON	Air Group 82—37 Hellcats, 37 Corsairs, 15 Helldivers, 15 Avengers
ESSEX	Air Group 83—36 Hellcats, 36 Corsairs, 15 Helldivers, 15 Avengers
HANCOCK	Air Group 6—72 Hellcats, 12 Helldivers, 10 Avengers
RANDOLPH	Air Group 12—57 Hellcats, 15 Helldivers, 15 Avengers
WASP	Air Group 86—34 Hellcats, 15 Helldivers, 15 Avengers, 36 Corsairs
YORKTOWN	Air Group 9 —40 Hellcats, 33 Hellcat (fighter bomber), 15 Helldivers, 7 Avengers

Light Carriers

BATAAN	Air Group 47—24 Hellcats, 12 Avengers
BELLEAU WOOD	Air Group 30—25 Hellcats, 9 Avengers
COWPENS	Air Group 22—25 Hellcats, 9 Avengers
INDEPENDENCE	Air Group 46—25 Hellcats, 8 Avengers
MONTEREY	Air Group 28—25 Hellcats, 9 Avengers
SAN JACINTO	Air Group 45—25 Hellcats, 9 Avengers

Night Carrier Group — TG 38.4

BON HOMME RICHARD Air Group - — - Hellcats, - Avengers

Sweeps over the enemy airfields on 9th August, resulted in the destruction of over 50 Japanese aircraft by the RN aircraft, the latter losing seven aircraft and five pilots.

The 10th August had been scheduled as the last full day of operations and the carrier aircraft roamed at will over Honshu, destroying what remained to the enemy of his aircraft, shipping and railway system. TF 37's share was over 50 enemy aircraft destroyed on the ground, three destroyers sunk and three more seriously damaged at Maizuru and in the Inland Sea, damage to factories shipyards and barracks. Altogether the enemy lost over 700 aircraft to the strikes of the Fast Carrier Force on 9th and 10th August 1945, and Royal Navy aircraft losses for the two days were 13 aircraft and nine crews. The Kamikazes made their only appearances during these two days; improved defensive techniques denied them any success bar the damaging of a picket destroyer, while the CAP, usually over 100 strong, shot down the majority of the enemy aircraft venturing out.

Owing to delays in the actual details of the surrender being worked out, the BPF was asked to contribute one more day's operations, but after RAS on 11th the weather was too bad for strikes. Regretfully, the main strength, VICTORIOUS, FORMIDABLE and IMPLACABLE had to return to Sydney, leaving a token force, INDEFATIGABLE, KING GEORGE V, GAMBIA, NEWFOUNDLAND and 10 destroyers as Task Group 38.5, under the direct command of Admiral McCain.

On 13th August the air attacks were directed at the Tokyo area once more, only targets of opportunity remaining, so effective had been the strikes during the preceding month. In the course of the last large-scale attacks on the carrier forces, the CAP shot down another 21 Japanese aircraft, the Seafires destroying five of these. Aware that surrender

was near, Task Force 38 withdrew to refuel, but in the absence of notifi-
cation of the cease-fire further operations were laid on for 15th. The
dawn strikes were launched, and INDEFATIGABLE's Avengers were
intercepted by a dozen A6Ms and in the last fighter combat of World
War II the Seafires of No. 24 Naval Fighter Wing shot down eight of the
enemy for the loss of just one Seafire. Most of the remainder of the
enemy fighters were damaged in the encounter.

All further strikes were cancelled at 0700 on 15th August, and only a
few die-hard Japanese attempted to attack the Fleet, INDEFATIGABLE
being near-missed. The Royal Navy contingent remained with the
Fifth Fleet, replenished by the USN Fleet Train, until the signing of the
instrument of surrender in Tokyo Bay on 2nd September 1945.

The Carrier Squadron had been ably led throughout the existence
of the British Pacific Fleet by Admiral Vian. This distinguished officer
will be best remembered for his exploits in destroyers and with the 15th
Cruiser Squadron in the Mediterranean, but there is no doubt that his
drive and ready adaptability to the operational requirements of aircraft
carrier warfare led to the high standard displayed by the 21 squadrons
embarked in the six Fleet carriers which served under his command
in the East Indies and Pacific. Less than 50 Fleet Air Arm aircraft
were lost during these final operations off the Japanese Home Islands.

On VJ-Day there were four Light Fleet carriers at Sydney, with nearly
160 Barracudas and Corsairs embarked, preparing for operations in the
East Indies and Philippines. These four ships, the 11th Aircraft Carrier
Squadron, were given the task of re-occupation of British territories.
VENERABLE accompanied INDOMITABLE at Hong Kong, Rear
Admiral C. H. J. Harcourt, RN, flying his flag in the latter, where the
two ships launched the last offensive sorties against Japanese forces. On
31st August and 1st September, Corsairs, Hellcats, Avengers and Barra-

---

DISPOSITION OF VESSELS AND SQUADRONS

The 11th Aircraft Carrier Squadron— non-operational before 15th August 1945
VENERABLE — Flag Rear Admiral C. H. J. Harcourt RN
    1851 Squadron   21 Corsairs
    814   „   18 Barracudas
COLOSSUS
    1846 Squadron   24 Corsairs
    827   „   18 Barracudas
GLORY
    1831 Squadron   21 Corsairs
    837   „   18 Barracudas
VENGEANCE
    1850 Squadron   24 Corsairs
    812   „   18 Barracudas
Repair Carrier
UNICORN
Ferry and Replacement CVEs
    STRIKER   SLINGER   CHASER
    ARBITER   REAPER   SPEAKER
Working-up as Night C.A.P. CVE
VINDEX
    1790 Squadron   12 Firefly IIs

cudas dive-bombed and strafed suicide boats sortieing for a last attack, and went on to destroy those that remained hidden in the bays on the north of Hong Kong Island.

GLORY took General B. A. H. Sturdee of the Australian Army to Rabaul to accept the surrender of the Japanese in New Britain in early September, meeting no opposition.

After the last shots and final operations the British Pacific Fleet was soon dispersed. The Socialist Government had given undertakings that personnel would be returned for demobilisation as soon as possible, and the operational strength of the Fleet as a whole diminished as the most experienced men left. Two important tasks were left for the carriers. The vast available spaces of a carrier's hangar and flight deck were eminently suitable for the evacuation of ex-prisoners of war, and hundreds of thousands of these unfortunates were repatriated by the carriers of the BPF, 11th ACS, and CVE Service Squadron.

The other, rather sad, task of the carriers was the dumping of Lend-Lease aircraft at sea off Sydney. With thousands of Corsairs, Hellcats, Avengers, Wildcats and secondline types in the Naval Air Stations and Repair Yards, this process took many months, but under the terms of the Lend-Lease Agreement, which stipulated that aircraft retained had to be paid for; as the United States Navy did not wish the aircraft to be returned the waste was inevitable. A few Hellcats and Corsairs were retained until the autumn of 1946, embarked in the Light Fleet carriers. The majority of the Fleet carriers were in Home waters by the end of 1945, together with the CVEs, which were returned to the United States during the succeeding months.

The Royal Navy's aircraft carrier operations against the Imperial Japanese Navy, which had begun on a note of extreme caution in April 1942, developed into a thoroughly offensive means of prosecuting the War in the East, against an enemy whose fortunes depended upon the command of the oceans to a very great extent.

The full credit for destroying the IJN as a fighting force must go to the United States Navy. While the submarines of the Pacific Fleet inflicted a vast amount of damage on the enemy's merchant marine, the American carriers decimated his striking forces. In a succession of bitter air/sea battles; Coral Sea, Midway, the Eastern Solomons, Santa Cruz, the Philippine Sea, Cape Engaño and off Okinawa, carrier aircraft from USN ships sank 11 aircraft carriers, two battleships and a dozen cruisers, for the loss of four of their own carriers in these same battles. Strikes against enemy strongholds, such as Truk and Rabaul, resulted in further attrition—losses which the enemy could not make good with the over-extended lines of communication cut by the submarines and carrier task forces.

By the time that the Royal Navy was sufficiently strong to join the United States in a joint Allied Fleet, there were few large-scale battles to be fought. The carriers of the British Pacific Fleet proved themselves to be efficient units, flying as hard as their USN opposite numbers on sustained high intensity strike missions against airfields, shipping, and road and rail systems.

Appendices

U-boats sunk by Fleet Air Arm Aircraft

U- 64 : Swordfish floatplane from WARSPITE	— Rombaks Fjord 13/4/40
U-451 : Swordfish of 812 Squadron based at Gibraltar	— off Tangier 21/12/41
U-517 : Albacore of 817 Squadron from VICTORIOUS	— mid-Atlantic 21/11/42
U-752 : Swordfish of 819 Squadron from ARCHER	— Atlantic convoy 23/5/43
U-666 : Swordfish of 842 Squadron from FENCER	— Atlantic convoy 10/2/44
U-366 : Swordfish of 816 Squadron from CHASER	— Arctic convoy 5/3/44
U-973 : Swordfish of 816 Squadron from CHASER	— Arctic convoy 6/3/44
U-288 : Swordfish of 819 Squadron from ACTIVITY and Avengers of 846 Squadron from TRACKER	— Arctic convoy 3/4/44
U-277 : Swordfish of 842 Squadron from FENCER	— Arctic convoy 1/5/44
U-674 : Swordfish of 842 Squadron from FENCER	— Arctic convoy 2/5/44
U-959 : Swordfish of 842 Squadron from FENCER	— Arctic convoy 2/5/44
U-354 : Swordfish of 825 Squadron from VINDEX	— Arctic convoy 25/8/44
U-921 : Swordfish of 813 Squadron from CAMPANIA	— Arctic convoy 30/9/44
U-365 : Swordfish of 813 Squadron from CAMPANIA	— Arctic convoy 13/12/44
U-711 : Avengers of 846 Squadron from TRUMPETER	— strike on Kilbotn 4/5/45

Vichy French Submarines sunk by Fleet Air Arm Aircraft

BEVEZIERS : Swordfish of 829 Squadron from ILLUSTRIOUS—Diego Suarez 5/5/42
LE HEROS : Swordfish of 829 Squadron from ILLUSTRIOUS—Diego Suarez 6/5/42

Vichy French Submarine shared with surface escort

PONCELET : Walrus from DEVONSHIRE with sloop MILFORD — Cameroons 9/11/40

U-boats shared with surface escorts and other Services

U-131 :	Martlets of 802 Squadron from AUDACITY with EXMOOR, BLANKNEY, STANLEY, STORK and PENSTEMON	— Gibraltar convoy — 17/12/41
U-589 :	Swordfish of 825 Squadron from AVENGER with ONSLOW	— Arctic convoy — 14/9/42
U-331 :	Albacore of 820 Squadron from FORMID-ABLE with Coastal Command Hudsons	— off Algerian coast — 17/11/42
U-203 :	Swordfish of 811 Squadron from BITER with PATHFINDER	— Atlantic convoy — 25/4/43
U- 89 :	Swordfish of 811 Squadron from BITER with BROADWAY and LAGAN	— Atlantic convoy — 12/5/43
U-472 :	Swordfish of 816 Squadron from CHASER with ONSLAUGHT	— Arctic convoy — 4/3/44
U-653 :	Swordfish of 825 Squadron from VINDEX with STARLING and WILD GOOSE	— Atlantic A/S Sweep — 15/3/44
U-355 :	Avenger of 846 Squadron from TRACKER with BEAGLE	— Arctic convoy — 1/4/44

U-765 : Swordfish of 825 Squadron from VINDEX — Atlantic A/S Sweep
         with AYLMER, BICKERTON and BLIGH   — 6/5/44

U-198 : Avengers of 832 Sqdn (BEGUM) and 851 —
         Sdqn (SHAH) with FINDHORN and RIndN   — Indian Ocean A/S Sweep
         GODAVARI   — 12/8/44

U-344 : Swordfish of 825 Squadron from VINDEX
         with MERMAID, PEACOCK, KEPPEL and   — Arctic convoy
         LOCH DUNVEGAN   — 24/8/44

U-394 : Swordfish of 825 Squadron from VINDEX — Arctic convoy
         with MERMAID, PEACOCK and KEPPEL   — 2/9/44

U-1060 : Barracudas of No. 2 TBR Wing from
         IMPLACABLE, bombed when beached by   — Strike on Rorvik
         311 and 502 Squadrons   — 27/10/44

         SWORDFISH — 12½ "outright" kills
                        8   shared kills

         AVENGERS   —   1½ "outright" kills
                        2   shared kills

         ALBACORES —   1 "outright" kill
                        1   shared kill

         MARTLET and BARRACUDA — 1 shared kill each

THE AIRCRAFT CARRIERS

At the outbreak of War in September 1939 the aircraft carrier was, figuratively, still in its adolescence. Although FURIOUS had undertaken the first carrier operations in July 1918, the first carrier with a full-length flight deck, ARGUS, did not become operational until after the end of World War I. Over the next 10 years another four carriers joined the Fleet, and there was then a delay of another 10 years before the first of the modern ships, ARK ROYAL, entered service. Apart from the budgetary considerations, more rapid expansion proved impractical until the techniques of deck-work and ship-handling had been worked out in service. One example of the lengthy gestatory period of equipment for the carriers was the development of the arrester gear—not until 1933 were the transverse wires now accepted as logical adopted for full use. ARK's two catapults were the first to be installed in a British carrier, although catapults had been installed in cruisers for some years by the time she entered service, in November 1938. The safety barrier, designed to protect aircraft in the forward deck-park from the possibility of damage from an aircraft missing the wires and over-running while landing, did not become standard until 1940. The practice prior to that time had been to strike each aircraft down the lifts after land-on before recovering the next, a time-consuming exercise.

The Royal Navy possessed a total of six front-line Fleet carriers in 1939, only two of which, HERMES and ARK ROYAL, had been designed as such. FURIOUS, GLORIOUS and COURAGEOUS were conversions from World War I battle-cruisers, while EAGLE was laid down as a battleship and completed as a carrier. The remaining ship, ARGUS, was a conversion from a luxury liner, and was regarded as being too slow, small, and ill-protected for Fleet employment. Used largely for ferry operations, ARGUS was not used as a front-line carrier until after the loss of ARK ROYAL in November 1941.

One feature shared by all the British ships was the integral design of the hangar, which was within the structure of the ship, rather than forming part of a vast super-structure, together with the associated flight deck and lifts, as in the American and Japanese carriers. The hangar in the Royal Navy's carriers was a box, with no apertures in the deck, and only the lift shafts breaking the deck-head, formed in most cases by the flight deck. On either side of the hangar, access was gained through flashproof lobbies with workshops and mess-decks filling the remainder of the space so that the hangar walls never formed the sides of the ship. With good extractor fans exhausting straight through to the outside air, the dangerous aviation gasoline fumes constituted no hazard to the remainder of the ship and no British-*built* ship was lost as the result of a petrol explosion or hangar fire. In the case of the carriers with two hangar decks, a fire could be contained by the steel or asbestos fire-curtains, whatever the position of the lifts. The later armoured carriers took the standards of protection to the high standards which exist today.

The standard of internal sub-division in the pre-War carriers was not of such a high standard as the fire precautions. GLORIOUS and HERMES were sunk by gunfire and bombing respectively, against which they had little horizontal protection, while COURAGEOUS and EAGLE were both lost to submarine torpedo attack, going down in a matter of minutes with heavy loss of life, after inadequate damage control capacity had been unable to deal with the inflow of water. ARK ROYAL's protection was somewhat better, but she too was lost to torpedo attack, the main cause of her loss being a fire in the one serviceable boiler-room, which deprived her of pump pressure, which had been coping with the buoyancy problem up to that time. FURIOUS and ARGUS were the sole survivors of the pre-War carriers, both surviving air attack without receiving a direct hit and, as far as is known, never attacked by submarine. ARGUS was withdrawn from active service at the beginning of 1943 and used for deck-landing training until mid-1944, while FURIOUS, which had seen a considerable amount of service, both with the Home Fleet and in the Mediterranean, was reduced to reserve in September 1944.

The armoured carriers were laid down before the War and incorporated the many improvements developed over the previous 15 years, most of which had appeared in ARK ROYAL. The large starboard-side island with a single funnel, first seen in HERMES, was standard by this time, only ARGUS and FURIOUS being flush-decked, and the flight deck overhung the hull, with which it formed a "clean" shape, with enclosed bow and stern.   In common with ARK, the new ships were armed with 16 × 4.5in dual-purpose guns, mounted in paired, counter-sunk turrets at the "corners" of the ship, slightly below deck-level.   The first 4 ships also shared the same, unusual, machinery arrangements as ARK, 3 shafts being driven by 3 engine-rooms and boiler-rooms, giving a speed in excess of 31 knots.

The principal difference between the ILLUSTRIOUS-class and all other aircraft carriers lay in the design philosophy.   Aircraft complement was sacrificed to protection, particularly from air attack.   The hangar became an armoured box, with a 3-4in flight-deck, 2½in hangar deck, and no less than 4½in of armour in the hangar sides.   With a displacement of 22,600 tons, nearly 1,000 tons more than ARK ROYAL, the later ships were 50 feet shorter and, with only one hangar deck, could only carry half the number of aircraft.   The reduced aircraft complement was of less tactical significance than would seem to be the case, as only a limited number of aircraft could be ranged for one launch, about 15 by ILLUSTRIOUS and 20 by ARK ROYAL.   Not until the adoption of the "tail-down" catapult launching technique could a large number of aircraft be launched for a strike, and by then, circa 1943, improved stowage arrangements had almost doubled the aircraft capacity of the armoured carriers.

The logistic consideration was greater.   In areas where the Fleet Air Arm aircraft supply situation was tenuous, the smaller aircraft complement resulted in an inadequate reserve of front-line aircraft to counter attrition, and very often the embarked aircraft represented the entire FAA strength in overseas theatres of operations.

The first three armoured carriers, ILLUSTRIOUS, FORMIDABLE and VICTORIOUS, were the only ships to have just the one hangar, served by 2 small lifts fore and aft and themselves armoured to the strength of the rest of the deck.   INDOMITABLE was altered while building to feature a half-hangar aft below the full-length hangar, served by the after lift only.   The extra space was sufficient to accommodate an extra squadron.   In the last two ships to be completed before the end of the War, INDEFATIGABLE and IMPLACABLE, the design was taken a stage further and these both had two full-length hangars.   Their length over-all went up by only 16 feet, and the tonnage by 3,400 tons, but the extra space allowed for double the aircraft complement of the ILLUSTRIOUS-class, at the expense of the hangar side-wall armour.

The Fleet carriers saw world-wide service and proved to be very efficient ships, capable of absorbing a frightening amount of damage.   All but IMPLACABLE were hit by enemy action : in January 1941 ILLUSTRIOUS survived what was probably the heaviest damage inflicted on an Allied ship at sea.   FORMIDABLE and INDOMITABLE also suffered heavy bomb damage in the Mediterranean, while VICTORIOUS was hit by a heavy bomb which broke up on the armoured deck. There was less underwater protection, both INDOMITABLE and FORMIDABLE suffering from heavy damage below the water-line from very near-misses.   The former was the only one of her type to be torpedoed, and again the underwater damage was considerable, resulting in over a year away from operations.   The list of American and Japanese ships lost to bombing and torpedo attack, after far fewer hits and apparently insignificant damage, is too long to be covered here, but suffice to say that the lack of an armoured deck and sealed hangar system gave them less chance of survival.   (TAIHO, a Japanese Fleet carrier with a marked external resemblance to INDOMITABLE, was built with an armoured deck, but the open hangar design allowed inflammable vapours to permeate the entire ship, resulting in her loss through fire and explosion).

Four of the Fleet carriers were hit by Kamikaze during the operations off the Sakishima Gunto in April and May 1945, but in only one example was the flight deck holed, by a splinter, and all were back in action within a matter of a few hours. The American ESSEX-class carriers, rather larger and with a greater aircraft complement (100 plus) generally required months in a dockyard following bomb or Kamikaze damage, although none was actually lost during the class's two years of combat operations.

The only other class of Fleet carrier to enter service before the end of the War was the Light Fleet design.   The COLOSSUS-class was unarmoured, and their hulls were built to Lloyds specification up to the main deck, the idea being to convert them to merchant ships after the War.   The vertical sub-division was on a much less comprehensive scale than in the Fleet carriers, and the Light Fleets displaced only 13,000 tons. With a flight deck length of about 690 feet, they were appreciably smaller than the ILLUSTRIOUS and her sisters, but were capable of operating 40-odd aircraft. The main shortcoming of the Light Fleet carriers was their relative lack of speed. With only a third of the horse-power available to the larger ships, they were hard-pressed to make their designed 25 knots, although their cruising radius was significantly greater. Defensive armament consisted of close-range weapons only, long and medium-range defence of the ships being vested in their own aircraft and the guns of the screening escorts. None of the class saw action before the official cease-fire in the Pacific although aircraft from VENERABLE did sink some suicide boats off Hong Kong at the end of August 1945. None of the ships was converted for merchant service after the War, the design proving to be a useful compromise between efficiency and economy for peace-time service. Of the eight Light Fleet carriers of the COLOSSUS-class, four are still in service, in much modified form, with smaller navies, none of the others being scrapped before 1961. Only one of the armoured carriers survived into the 'sixties, VICTORIOUS, which was re-built for the operation of second-generation jet aircraft and was not withdrawn from front-line service until the end of 1967.

A total of three Maintenance carriers was completed during the War. UNICORN was designed as such, with 2 hangar decks and extensive repair facilities for the support of a carrier task force far from a main Fleet base. She saw front-line service off Salerno and escorting a couple of Gibraltar convoys, but from the end of 1943 UNICORN was stationed first with the Eastern Fleet at Trincomalee and latterly with the British Pacific Fleet Train. The other Maintenance carriers, PERSEUS and PIONEER, were converted from the Light Fleet design but neither joined the BPF in time to become fully operational before the end of the War. All the smaller carriers enjoyed the same standards of hangar design as their Fleet contemporaries, the Admiralty rightly believing that no saving in space and weight was worth the reduced safety margin.

THE ESCORT CARRIERS

The most numerous type of aircraft carrier to see action with both Royal and United States Navies was the escort carrier, converted from merchant hulls, complete, under construction, or adapted from the keel up. The conversions, simple at first, became more complex and sophisticated as the War progressed and the disadvantages of the early ships became apparent.

Although the concept of such conversions dated back to the early 'thirties, when the Naval Staff were considering means of augmenting carrier strength in the event of war, the first "auxiliary" carrier did not commence operations until September 1941, a full two years after the outbreak of War. An ex-German prize, EMPIRE AUDACITY (ex-HANNOVER), was fitted with the barest essentials for the operation of half-a-dozen Martlet fighters and in the course of just four months of convoy escort on the Gibraltar run, AUDACITY demonstrated the value of continuous daylight air cover for the protection of merchant ships in convoy. In addition to the destruction of several shadowers, her aircraft sighted and drove down several U-boats, which would otherwise have been able to reach an attacking position— an example of the negative side of A/S success.

Despite the success of this small fighter carrier, which enjoyed primitive operating conditions only parallelled by those in the MAC-ships, only four other British-built escort carriers became fully operational during the War. The Ministry of War Transport was loth to release the large, fast ships of the type required for conversion, apparently not fully appreciating what subsequent events were to prove, namely that the saving of merchant shipping under close carrier escort would have fully justified the sacrifice of the freight-carrying capacity of those ships converted to the escort carrier role.

Thus it was that the bulk of the escort carriers to serve with the Royal Navy were built in the United States, where the prototype CVE, LONG ISLAND, had entered service shortly before Pearl Harbour. An almost identical sister-ship, ARCHER, was ordered for the Royal Navy, together with four other vessels which differed from her only in displacement and propulsion details. All were diesel-powered and had a wooden flight deck with just one lift, serving a hangar which occupied approximately half the length of the ship. One CVE, CHARGER, was retained by the USN for training, but the other four vessels began operations with the Royal Navy during 1942. The first to see action was AVENGER, with a North Russian convoy in September 1942, and the other two ships of her class joined her for the invasion of North Africa in the following November. ARCHER, as related in the text, was plagued with machinery defects and saw only brief operational service on trade protection in the summer of 1943.

Following American practice, the CVEs were all built with wooden flight decks, which had certain advantages over the steel deck invariably featured in British ships, and with "open" hangars. The fuel and fire protection standards did not match up to the high standards laid down by the Admiralty, and after the loss of AVENGER, to a single submarine torpedo, and the tragic explosion in DASHER, an intensive modification programme was applied to every CVE on arrival in the United Kingdom. The modifications included the addition of nearly 2,000 tons of ballast and a complete revision of the aviation fuel and bomb stowage systems. As a result of the improvements the ships were generally more stable than their USN opposite numbers, who preferred to ballast with sea water as tanks emptied. Two modified CVEs were damaged by U-boat torpedo and survived, while AMEER was hit by a Kamikaze and returned to operations within a month. By contrast, both USN escort carriers to be torpedoed sank quickly, with heavy loss of life, and of the 10 hit by Kamikaze, two were lost and the others damaged beyond economical wartime repair.

All CVEs delivered subsequent to the first four were adaptations of the standard C-3 hull, and were powered by a single-shaft geared turbine, which often tended to be troublesome in service, due partly to the inexperience of the Merchant Navy engine-room staff who served in all these ships, but more to the fact that at that time the turbine was not the most suitable engine for mass-production techniques. The ATTACKER-class corresponded to the USN BOGUE-class, the RULER-class having much the same characteristics, but with a slightly larger aircraft complement. As many as 30 of the smaller fighter types could be carried, or about 12-16 strike aircraft. An advantage of the unarmoured design was that the aircraft lifts were considerably larger than in the Fleet carriers, permitting the easy stowage of aircraft with non-folding wings, such as the Sea Hurricane and Seafire IIC. A catapult was installed in all the ships after the first four, although certain British aircraft types were unable to take advantage of the facility as they had been designed for the earlier British "accelerator", with its "tail-up" launching configuration.

At a fairly early stage the CVEs were divided into two broad operational categories, with slightly different equipment outfits to suit them for the roles. Trade protection escort carriers carried a less elaborate radar system than the Assault carriers, but were fitted with HF/DF equipment to allow them to supplement the information available to the Escort Group Commander. The operations organisation was directed more towards a surface action, or A/S action, than in the Assault CVEs, which concentrated more on air interception and planning and briefing of close air support missions. Certain of the Trade Protection ships were "Arcticised" for winter operations in polar latitudes.

The Assault carriers operated only fighter types and were equipped with a small but comprehensive fighter direction system in addition to more spacious briefing and intelligence rooms. Although AVENGER, BITER and DASHER operated in the Assault role off Algeria in November 1942, the first action by CVEs fitted out for the task was not until the following September, off Salerno. The Fighter CVEs PURSUER, SEARCHER and ATHELING, were equipped in the same fashion as the Assault ships, being intended originally for the fighter protection of Gibraltar convoys. As it was apparent that the trade protection carriers' fighter flights were fully capable of providing this cover, the Fighter CVEs were used rather as Assault carriers. PURSUER did sail with a couple of round-voyage convoys, however, scoring a notably victory in February 1944. ATHELING was employed operationally only briefly, in the Indian Ocean, in the summer of 1944.

The escort carriers met with immediate success in their introduction to anti-submarine operations, but not until the spring of 1944 were they used for offensive strike action as a routine task. Both Trade Protection and Assault CVEs saw considerable action off the Norwegian coast, between April 1945 and May 1945.

Avenger-armed ships laid all the Navy's air-dropped mines in the Leads, apart from one operation by PUNCHER's Barracudas. Hellcats and Wildcats from Assault CVEs provided the bulk of the fighter escort for the shipping strikes, minelaying and the attacks on the TIRPITZ. After October 1943, the CVEs were the only carriers deployed operationally in the Mediterranean, their main operations taking place between August and October 1944. A similar situation existed in the East Indies after the beginning of 1945, when the Fleet carriers departed for the Pacific. The 21st Aircraft Carrier Squadron consisted entirely of CVEs, 14 being on strength at the end of the War in the East. On 2nd May 1945, there were 11 CVEs at sea, in action or en route for an operation, with as many more working-up or on passage.

A large number of CVEs were never used operationally, being employed for ferrying. Up to 70 aircraft could be carried by a ferry carrier, for delivery to the United Kingdom, or as replacement aircraft for the BPF or Eastern Fleet. Not only naval aircraft were ferried: as the USAAF in Europe increased in size, so the shorter-ranged aircraft were brought across in growing numbers, while many RAF aircraft were taken out to India and Burma by the CVEs.

The four British-built escort carriers to see action, ACTIVITY, NAIRANA, VINDEX and CAMPANIA all entered service after the beginning of 1944 and scored many successes between them in Arctic waters. Built to Admiralty standards, they incorporated the fully integral hangars of the Fleet units with the results that their operational complement was generally less than 18 Swordfish and Wildcats. All had unarmoured steel flight decks and were powered by 2-shaft diesels, giving speeds in the region of 18-19 knots, slightly faster than their smaller American counterparts. The largest British-built escort carrier was PRETORIA CASTLE, converted from a Union Castle liner, which was used only for training and trials in Home Waters.

At the end of the War all the American ships were returned to the USN after employment on repatriation duties all over the world. The last to be returned were RAJAH and PATROLLER, handed over on 13th December 1946. Of the British ships, NAIRANA was sold to the Royal Netherlands Navy and CAMPANIA was retained by the RN, finally being scrapped in 1955, after conversion to a floating exhibition, as part of the 1951 Festival of Britain.

Altogether 48 aircraft carriers were operational with the Royal Navy, from first to last, eight of these being sunk. Two more were damaged beyond repair by enemy action, two wore themselves out through continuous service, one had to be laid up due to persistent defects, and another was badly damaged in collision and not returned to service.

Pre-War Fleet Carriers (the order is that of initial commissioning for aircraft carrier operations)

ARGUS	employed on Deck Landing Training to June 1940, ferry operations to December 1941, DLT 1943 to 1944
EAGLE	operational to the time of her loss: torpedoed by U-73 on 11th August 1942
HERMES	operational: sunk by dive-bombers from AKAGI, SORYU, HIRYU, on 9th April 1942
COURAGEOUS	operational: torpedoed by U-29 on 17th September 1939
GLORIOUS	operational & ferry duties: sunk by gunfire of SCHARNHORST and GNEISENAU on 8th June 1940
FURIOUS	operational until reduced to reserve in September 1944
ARK ROYAL	operational: torpedoed by U-81 on 13 November 1941, sank while under tow on the following day

Armoured Carriers

ILLUSTRIOUS	operational from end of August 1940; badly damaged 10/1/41; near-missed by Kamikaze 6th April 1945; under long re-fit at the end of the War
FORMIDABLE	operational from November 1940; badly damaged 26/5/41; hit by Kamikaze 4th and 9th May 1945; operational at end of War
VICTORIOUS	operational from May 1941; hit by Kamikaze (2) 9th May 1945; operational at end of War

INDOMITABLE   operational from December 1941; badly damaged 12th August
               1942 and again on 11th July 1943; hit by Kamikaze 4th May
               1945; under short re-fit at end of War
INDEFATIGABLE operational July 1944; hit by Kamikaze 1st April 1945; opera-
               tional at end of War
IMPLACABLE   operational October 1944 to end of the War

Light Fleet Carriers Eleventh Aircraft Carrier Squadron

VENERABLE   operational August 1945; only action was off Hong Kong;
               became Royal Netherlands Navy KAREL DOORMAN
COLOSSUS   non-operational; became French ARROMANCHES
GLORY   operational August 1945; no action; retained by RN
VENGEANCE   non-operational; to Royal Australian Navy; became Brazilian
               MINAS GERAIS

Repair and Maintenance Carriers

UNICORN   operational July-October 1943; maintenance task to end of War
PERSEUS   to BPF, summer 1945
PIONEER   to BPF, August 1945

Escort carriers—Trade protection (in order of entry into front-line service)

AUDACITY	torpedoed by U-741, 21st December 1941	NABOB	damaged by U-354, 22nd August 1944
AVENGER	torpedoed by U-155, 15th November 1942	TRUMPETER ATHELING	
BITER	to France, January 1945	BEGUM	
DASHER	blew up 27th March 1943	SHAH	
TRACKER	damaged in collision June 1944	PREMIER	
FENCER		PUNCHER	
BATTLER		QUEEN	
CHASER		EMPRESS	mainly employed as Assault CVE
STRIKER		SMITER	operational August 1945
ACTIVITY			no action
VINDEX			
NAIRANA			
CAMPANIA			

Assault and Fighter Escort Carriers

ATTACKER		EMPEROR	
HUNTER		KHEDIVE	
STALKER		AMEER	damaged by Kamikaze 26th July 1945
PURSUER			
SEARCHER		EMPRESS	
THANE	damaged by U-482 off Clyde, 15th January 1945	SPEAKER	with TF 112, April to May 1945
		RULER	with TF 112, Mar to August 1945

CVEs employed primarily on aircraft transport duties

PATROLLER   ARBITER
REAPER   RAJAH
SLINGER   RANEE
TROUNCER

Note: The majority of all CVEs did at least one ferry mission, in addition to ferrying
undertaken while on passage from one operational area to another

Training Escort Carriers

RAVAGER   PRETORIA CASTLE
    Full details of all the aircraft carriers are to be found in "Warships of World War II",
by H. T. Lenton and J. J. Colledge, published by Ian Allan Ltd.

Abbreviations

A-A	anti-aircraft (ack-ack) (usually friendly gunfire)
ACS	Aircraft Carrier Squadron
AoC	Air Officer Commanding (RAF)
A/S	anti-submarine
ASV	Air to Surface Vessel airborne radar
asdic	(Allied Submarine Detection Investigation Committee); an underwater radar, employing sound propagation for detection and ranging on underwater objects. Now known as 'sonar'—SOnic Azimuth and Ranging
BPF	British Pacific Fleet
CAM-ship	Catapult-Armed Merchantship (not commissioned as a warship)
Cant (Rd'A)	Cantieri Riuniti dell'Adriatico (Italian aeroplane manufacturer)
CAP	Combat Air Patrol
CVE	American-built escort carrier built on mercantile hull; USN designation (unofficially known as "Woolworth" or "Jeep") carriers
DLT	Deck Landing Training
FAA	Fleet Air Arm
FCS	Fighter Catapult Ship (commissioned as a warship)
FEAF	Far East Air Force (RAF)
flak	anti-aircraft gunfire (Flieger Abwehr Kanone) (usually enemy gunfire)
grt	gross registered tons/tonnage
MAC-ship	Merchant Aircraft Carrier (not commissioned as a warship)
MEAF	Middle East Air Force (RAF)
MTB	Motor Torpedo Boat
radar	RAdio Direction And Range (originally American, but adopted by British Services in place of RDF—Radio Direction Finding)
RAS	Replenishment At Sea
TBR	Torpedo, Bomber, Reconnaissance (aircraft)
TF	Task Force
TSR	Torpedo, Spotter, Reconnaissance (aircraft)
USN	United States Navy

185

Index of Warship Names

(References to illustrations are in italics)

186

General Index